Talib Choudhry

Photographs by
Ingrid Rasmussen

Thames & Hudson

The New
Creative
Home

LONDON STYLE

CONTENTS

Introduction 16

Chris Dyson 24
Owen Pacey 34
Alice Gomme 44
Nina Litchfield 52
Caroline Legrand 62
Alex Eagle 72
Jessica McCormack 82
Francis Sultana 92
Matilda Goad 100
Lee Broom 108
Hubert Zandberg 116
Laura Myers 130
Clements Ribeiro 140
Basso & Brooke 148

Carina Cooper 158
Gillian Hyland 168
Adam Brown 178
Matthew Williamson 188
Nikki Tibbles 198
Camille Walala 210
Rebecca Louise Law 220
Serafina Sama 230
Kevin Torre 240
Sophie Ashby 250
Daniela Cecilio 260
Hayley Newstead 268
Fyodor Golan 278

Directory 286

INTRODUCTION

Being invited into the homes of inspiring people in the world's most creatively vibrant city means seeing first-hand the transformative power of design – from the thoughtful application of a tin of paint to the architectural reinvention of a centuries-old building.

This high–low mix and cosmopolitan energy are what make London such a dynamic, pragmatic city. As waves of gentrification transform neighbourhoods, new creative enclaves pop up elsewhere.

The strikingly individual homes shown here provide a visual feast, but first, here is some food for thought – a few decorating wisdoms gleaned along the way. They are not rules, merely suggestions. As fashion designer Christopher Brooke (p. 148) says: 'Fortune favours the brave. If you learn the rules well, you'll have a greater advantage when it comes to breaking them.'

BE FEARLESS

Those of us who have agonized over multiple paint testers of virtually the same shade of white or allowed decorating indecision to result in an anodyne room should take a leaf out of Caroline Legrand's gilded book.

'I've learned not to be scared,' says the interior designer, whose Holland Park home (p. 62) is darkly glamorous and anything but tame. 'You just have to be daring and try things. The worst that can happen is that you have to replace something or give it another coat of paint. When you begin to think too much, that's when things start to go wrong.'

Perhaps the real point here is that there is no 'right' or 'wrong' when it comes to decorating, only things that you instinctively like or don't. So do what you like!

HOME IS WHERE THE ART IS

Of all the homes we visited, the apartments of interior designer Sophie Ashby (p. 250) and style-setter Alex Eagle (p. 72) resonated most. They felt aspirational yet achievable,

OPPOSITE Layered patterns in the eye-popping home of Camille Walala.

and underlined the importance of adding art interest to a space. 'When I design a room I start with an artwork and take inspiration from the colours,' Sophie says.

She sources original photography, paintings and sculpture for her work, but has taken a thriftier approach in her own flat. Framed posters, inexpensive prints and pages from secondhand books all feature in the wall of art above her sofa.

SMALL DETAILS, BIG DIFFERENCE

Stylist Matilda Goad's West London flat (p. 100) is small but perfectly formed, channelling old-fashioned charm. She has filled it with small, elegant touches, including plenty of flowers.

'I love making the atmosphere feel special,' she says. 'Whether we're having friends over or not, playing music and using our favourite glasses always lifts the mood. Adding beautiful candles and crisp linen feels like such a luxury at the end of a long day.'

PLAY AND DISPLAY

Artist Camille Walala's apartment (p. 210) is full of look-at-me colour and pattern. Her graphic patterns are writ large across walls, floors and fabrics. It's bold, bright and a bit bonkers, demonstrating just how far a little imagination can go.

But the most striking Cinderella space – an unpromising nook elevated to the exceptional – is the stairwell in architect Chris Dyson's Spitalfields townhouse (p. 24) – although designer Lee Broom's basement cinema room (p. 108) comes a close second. It serves as a gallery space, where a suspended kinetic sculpture refracts rainbows as it slowly twirls.

Through the first-floor landing window can be glimpsed a classical bust, unexpectedly prettifying the urban view.

'Displaying my artefacts makes the place feel bigger, more interesting and full of surprises,' Chris says. 'We change art within the space regularly, otherwise it becomes something that you don't really look at.'

INTO THE BLUE

Oh Nina, what lovely blue walls you have ... It's impossible not to be seduced by Nina Litchfield's deep-navy sitting room (p. 52). The walls are painted in Farrow & Ball's 'Hague Blue', which makes tasteful grey seem suddenly passé.

ABOVE RIGHT An oversized German railway clock in designer Lee Broom's sleek and spectacular flat.

There is no 'right' or 'wrong' when it comes to decorating, only things you instinctively like or don't.

'Everyone thought I was mad when I said I was going to paint it navy blue, but now it's the talking point,' Nina says. 'It's so cosy and draws people in. I haven't met one person yet who doesn't like the room. It's never dark – it's quite bright and beautiful.' Inky blue, it seems, is the new neutral.

Fashion designer Matthew Williamson doesn't do neutrals, however; his rainbow-bright sitting room (p. 188) features canary-yellow paintwork, a turquoise velvet sofa and parrot-print wallpaper. Colour confidence at its ebullient best.

OBJECT LESSON

Hubert Zandberg's Ladbroke Grove home (p. 116) is awe-inspiring. It is chock-full of thousands of objects – from the prehistoric to the crisply contemporary – organized into carefully curated vignettes. While there are many extraordinary items (taxidermy monkeys, mammoth tusks, coyote fur throws), it's not the individual details that stay with you when you leave, but rather the overall look and how it made you feel (cocooned, calm, curious). And while Hubert is a prodigious collector with an eye for quality, he doesn't buy a piece for its individual intrinsic value – it is almost always seen as part of a bigger whole.

'It's the process that interests me,' he says. 'I believe that everything has an energy that comes with it. Bringing the different energies together can transform an object. Sometimes something will resist, and you have to move it and put it with something else. Or the minute you've placed an object, you almost can't wait to put it in a new context. I see what it does in this very busy environment, but what would it do on an old table by itself? That's what keeps an interior alive and vital.'

OPPOSITE Floral motifs bloom across furniture, carpets, walls and canvases at the home of florist Nikki Tibbles.

CHRIS DYSON

ARCHITECT

Chris Dyson has a talent for transforming unloved old buildings into stylish yet comfortable homes. It is his willingness to undertake renovation projects few others would touch that reaps the rewards: to find a diamond in the dirt, you have to be willing to get your hands dirty.

Chris bought his first home in Spitalfields, in East London, in 1996, when it was still somewhere that even squatters avoided. Undaunted, he turned an abandoned leather factory into a handsome family home after persuading the owner to sell it to him. Not that it was for sale – Chris contacted the Land Registry to find out who owned the boarded-up building and made an offer, a trick that he has pulled off twice since. He now lives in a nearby four-storey Georgian house with his wife Sarah and their two children.

Chris has worked on scores of historic listed buildings, and has a particular love of Georgian architecture. 'There's an intimacy and scale that works with human proportions,' he explains. 'Some architects think having acres of space is more important than having walls to display art on. I'm drawn to the sort of architecture that makes spaces for specific activities and times of day.'

The renovation work took a year, and although there were definite advantages to working on a project for himself, there were downsides, too. 'I never give myself enough time to think about things properly,' he explains. 'For other people you rationalize more and have meetings and plan things. When I'm building for myself, it evolves more as a gut response to things.'

Chris has used the architecture of the street as inspiration for the interior, layering

ABOVE LEFT AND RIGHT Chris designed the kitchen himself, with custom cabinets that allow plenty of room for his 'Willow' pattern china.

OPPOSITE In the dining room, wishbone chairs and rubber flooring provide a modern touch. Pivoting windows are a clever design solution, while also being in keeping with the style of the house.

THIS PAGE Surprisingly, the four-poster bed frame is from Ikea. The bedlinen is from Merci in Paris, while the tongue-and-groove panelling on the walls is a reinstated period feature.

OPPOSITE A stairwell at the top of the house has become something of a gallery space, hung with paintings by Chris's daughter Isabella, among others, kinetic artworks and intricate plaster mouldings.

THIS PAGE Chris continually creates interesting vistas and plays with proportion. 'I like displaying my artefacts,' he says. 'It makes the place feel bigger, more interesting and full of surprise.'

OPPOSITE Chris's favourite place to relax is the top-floor rear balcony: 'It's a great place to sit and read – it's very private. I enjoy looking out over the rooftops and it's got good sunlight.'

vintage finds (many from nearby Spitalfields market) and more contemporary designs against muted panelled walls, in keeping with the era of the building. 'I wanted to use calm, earthy colours, and am very inspired by Axel Vervoordt and his approach to decoration,' Chris says. 'I'm not big on soft furnishings and unnecessarily fussy details.'

To keep clutter to a minimum, Chris added storage by bringing the walls forward a little and creating concealed cupboards, which 'cut down on the visual noise of having open bookshelves'. That's not to say that the house is devoid of decorative objects: 'I like displaying my artefacts. It makes the place feel bigger, more interesting and full of surprises. We change the art regularly, otherwise it becomes something that you don't really register or look at. It just recedes into the background.'

Below a stairwell at the top of the house, hung with paintings by his artist daughter Isabella, a cantilevered staircase in solid oak snakes its way up to a new floor housing the kitchen and dining areas. In contrast to the rest of the house, the space is bright and modern with a practical rubber floor. Other contemporary takes on the traditional include windows with narrow timber frames that pivot, allowing the air to circulate and the family's two cats to get in and out.

'It's a new level, so it felt natural to decorate it in a contemporary way, rather than doing something more traditional,' Chris explains. With his respect for heritage buildings and knack for thoughtfully renovating them to suit contemporary life, he is providing a tasteful blueprint for 21st-century urban living.

OWEN PACEY

RECLAIMED FURNITURE DEALER

Very little in Owen Pacey's Shoreditch home was new when he bought it; in fact, some things are positively prehistoric, such as the baby dinosaur skull that sits on his kitchen countertop. The house is also home to his architectural salvage business, Renaissance London, on the ground floor.

'I get a real buzz from finding things that are unique and restoring them,' Owen explains. 'I like to mix up styles and eras to keep things interesting.'

It is his eye for the unusual that has won him a number of high-profile clients, from supermodels and rock stars to financial tsars – although everyone is welcome to explore the Tardis-like showroom, where antique fireplaces sit alongside Louis XIV mirrors, 1960s Italian lighting and all manner of curios. Upstairs, deep-grey walls provide a calm backdrop for a heady pick-and-mix of furniture and contemporary art.

Owen's home is located in a former public house, built in the 1850s, and needed extensive renovations to make it viable as a live–work space. 'It's been a labour of love,' he says. 'It had lain empty for 10 years before I bought it, and the roof needed replacing.

There were pigeons everywhere. We completely remodelled the space and raised the ceiling height on the upper floors, so we could accommodate more rooms.'

The most impressive new addition is a roof terrace with statuary, mature olive trees and strategically placed box hedging. This verdant pocket of calm is perched high above London's booming new tech-hub and

ABOVE LEFT During the renovation works, Owen opened up the door frames, adding panelled French doors and horn handles from Ochre.

ABOVE RIGHT AND OPPOSITE Antique statuary is dotted about the house, keeping watch on the rooftop terrace and in the hallway.

the constant stream of traffic on Old Street. 'It was all crack dens and hookers around here when I moved in 21 years ago,' he says. 'The transformation in Shoreditch has been fantastic. It's still so creative and vibrant.'

This is also an apt description of his home. At one end of the living room, an imposing 19th-century Italian fireplace provides a focal point and at the other, bold paintings by the Scottish artist Calum Colvin, whose work Owen collects, hang above a louche, 1970s sofa. Bibles and ecclesiastical tomes (bought from a convent) create a striking feature on the back wall, while the ornate gold side table is by Coco Chanel – one of the few pieces of furniture she designed.

The statement lighting in the room evolves as Owen finds new pieces and moves things back down to the showroom. A Venini glass chandelier and a 'Spider' chandelier by Carl Muylle are on show for now. 'There were only 16 of them ever made,' Owen says of the latter. 'I had four of them, and sold one to Soho House New York.'

The dining room also features a mix of pieces from different eras, with 1970s Italian furniture and French lighting. Ornate

ABOVE LEFT AND RIGHT Owen designed the kitchen himself, adding custom-made doors to Ikea carcasses. Along with the T-Rex skull, a striking fan by Luke Morgan provides a talking point. The gold side table in the living room is by Coco Chanel.

OPPOSITE The painting of Elizabeth Taylor above the fireplace is by Pure Evil. 'He graffitied the side of my building one night, so I went round to his studio to speak to him about it,' says Owen. 'He looked a bit worried, but I told him that I loved it.'

radiators run throughout the space and the eye-catching vase is vintage Murano. Of the 18th-century fireplace, Owen says, 'I bought it off a monk years ago and, would you believe it, he ripped me off.'

The Wharhol-esque painting of Elizabeth Taylor by urban artist Charles Uzzell-Edwards, who goes by the name of Pure Evil, is a more recent purchase. Somehow it all forms a sophisticated whole. 'I do like adding quirky bits and get offered unusual things from time to time,' he adds.

The secret to creating such a seductive design scheme? 'Confidence,' Owen says, supremely confidently. 'Just buy things you think are great and they'll go together.'

ABOVE LEFT Even the bathroom features a grand Georgian fireplace. A slick 'Ghost' mirror by Philippe Starck for Kartell and freestanding tub provide a contemporary contrast.

OPPOSITE In the bedroom, the 19th-century bed is from La Maison, and the richly patterned bedlinen was picked up from a bazaar in Istanbul. The mother-of-pearl light is a 1970s design by Verner Panton.

ALICE GOMME

ARTIST AND ANTIQUES DEALER

Alice Gomme isn't like most people when it comes to possessions. It's not that she lives in an ascetic or minimalistic way – quite the opposite – but rather that she's so used to acquiring things and then letting them go, she has a take-it-or-leave it approach to furnishing her flat.

'My home is like a travelling circus – exciting things appear and pass through each week.'

'For the first couple of months, I lived in the middle of the main room with just my mattress on the floor and loads of palm trees,' Alice says, sitting on a leather armchair in the now-furnished living area. 'Someday I might have to go back to that and ditch the stuff.'

But it's precisely all the 'stuff' that makes her flat in the North London neighbourhood of Kentish Town (perched above Primrose Hill and Camden Town) so intriguing. It hasn't been decorated so much as curated, with junk-shop finds and all manner of curios layered against the whitewashed walls. 'This is me trying to be minimal,' Alice says, 'but I'm not very good at it. My home is like a travelling circus – exciting things appear and pass through each week.'

The current star of the show is a wild boar's skeleton, which came from a museum in the Czech Republic and will soon be moving on to pastures new. But there are some constants among the haul; much of the furniture came from Alice's grandparents, who founded the iconic company G Plan in the 1950s. 'It's something that's just been passed down through the family,' she says. 'I've never chosen it, but I wouldn't part with it either.'

ABOVE The coffee table is an old lightbox, found abandoned in a field, while the colourful, naive paintings are by a friend, British artist Danny Fox.

OPPOSITE An ever-changing display of curios sit on low wooden benches. Old French shutters have been used as doors for a cupboard, and the wire table and smoked-glass lamp are both fleamarket finds.

Alice grew up on Portobello Road, browsing its fabled street market and antiques shops most days. 'It made me believe in the beauty and stories behind objects, and I just fell into antiques dealing myself,' she says.

Among her most cherished pieces are Inuit artefacts, because 'they combine purity of shape and material like nothing else'. Her love of nature can also be seen in the groupings of driftwood, stones and feathers, used to create unexpected tablescapes, and the profusion of leafy plants, which soften the industrial edge of the Victorian former school building.

Alice opened up the 140 m² (1,500 sq ft) flat as much as possible to let the light flow through it. 'Part of me wanted to feel like I was living outside,' she says. 'I had lived in so many basements before this, so it felt amazing to move into a space with so many big windows.'

One side of the flat faces a typical London street; the other looks out over a courtyard that has a more European feel, particularly on warm evenings. Inside, the kitchen table is the social hub for Alice and her revolving troupe of flatmates, but if unexpected guests arrive, they push it aside and sit on the floor.

'It's great living with friends who work like I do – erratically and creatively,' she says. 'Our home is always chaotic but fun.'

ABOVE LEFT AND RIGHT A nook between a window and Alice's darkroom has been turned into a mini-home office. In the kitchen, cupboards were removed in favour of rustic, open shelving.

OPPOSITE The vintage leather armchair is a G Plan piece that Alice inherited from her grandparents. Next to it, the skeleton of a wild boar came from a museum in the Czech Republic.

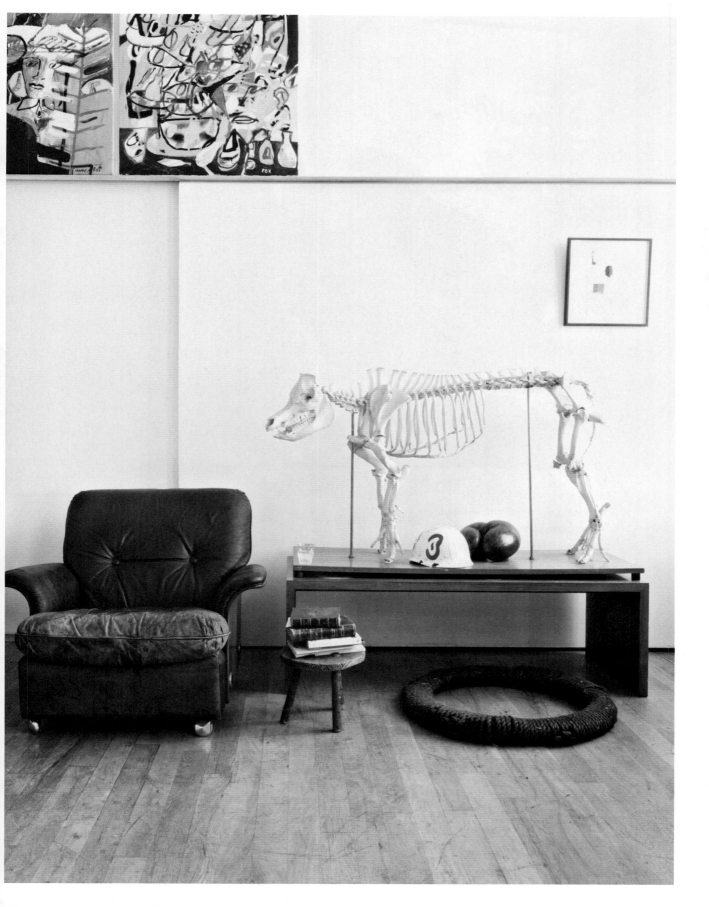

THIS PAGE Alice's love of nature can be seen in the groupings of driftwood, stones and feathers that have been used to create unexpected tablescapes.

OPPOSITE A framed tapestry from the former East Germany hangs in the bedroom. Alice found the rusty, clawfoot bath in Fens, a salvage shop on Lots Road. 'My biggest must-have is a huge bath,' she says. 'I'll never go without one again – winters are too long in the UK!'

NINA LITCHFIELD

INTERIOR DESIGNER

'Eclectic with a touch of timeless elegance,' is how Nina Litchfield describes her approach to decorating her stylish three-storey Victorian house in the heart of Notting Hill. 'I like to mix old and new,' she says, 'but I never want it to look as if I've tried too hard.'

This is also the perfect way to describe Nina herself – with her vintage fur coats and slick of red lipstick, there's something charmingly old-fashioned and glamorous about her. In the dramatic, dark-blue living room, she points out a portrait of her husband Vasco's grandmother.

'Margaret was an extraordinary, strong woman and a beautiful English rose,' she says. 'Her husband John was an officer in the British Navy and later became MP for Chelsea. I love having them both in the living room, watching over us.'

The room's dark colour had its detractors at first, but now, Nina says, 'I haven't met one person yet that doesn't comment positively and like the room. It's never dark – quite the opposite, it's bright and beautiful.'

The blue-and-white striped sofa is an antique piece that Nina has had since she married. 'We first had it upholstered in a flowery old fabric, which made it even more romantic and feminine. I loved it, but the fabrics began to wear out, so I needed to come up with a solution. I decided to revamp it completely and bring it into the 21st century

ABOVE The living-room walls are painted in 'Hague Blue' from Farrow & Ball: 'The room is so cosy, and everyone thought I was mad when I painted it navy blue. But now it's a talking point: it draws people in.'

OPPOSITE In the hallway, the traditional Victorian tiled floor contrasts with an old Dutch bench and artwork from Nicky Haslam's shop off Pimlico Road.

by mixing three different Designers Guild fabrics. They work in perfect harmony, and now I love it even more.'

As the couple have two young children, the house, despite being full of antique furniture and works of art, is very much a family home. Paintings by the children appear alongside those by more famous artists, and their books and toys are dotted around the place.

'A home needs to reflect the people who live there and to be comfortable,' Nina says. 'I don't like very stark interiors. The feeling of cosiness and warmth is very important to me.'

When the family moved into the house, it was anything but warm and had been painted white throughout to emphasize the generous proportions. No building work was needed, and Nina was able to begin adding character to the interior right away, using strong hits of colour, a mix of furniture from different

eras and eye-catching curios – including a tall palm tree in the lounge, which reflects her Brazilian–German heritage.

'Growing up with these two different cultures has definitely influenced the way I think and decorate,' explains Nina, who recently launched an interior-design business after studying at the illustrious Inchbald School of Design in Belgravia.

ABOVE RIGHT In the dining room, the oversized mirror is from Shane Meredith Antiques in Fulham and the walls are painted in 'Fowler Pink' by Farrow & Ball, while the cabinet and table are vintage Scandinavian pieces.

OPPOSITE The industrial-style metal stools were a wedding gift from interior designer Mimmi O'Connell. Much of the furniture came from antiques markets. 'I love vintage,' Nina says. 'It has so much character and always has a story to tell.'

'I like diversity in my interiors,' she adds. 'In Germany, you have the contrast of the old Baroque style and the Bauhaus era. Brazil is vibrant and colourful, with beautiful colonial buildings and Modernism thrown into the mix. I like to take ideas from these different influences to a make a space work.'

It goes some way to explaining her fearless approach to decorating. An antique French sofa reupholstered in bold blue and white stripes is a perfect example – the fabric, rather than overpowering the elegant silhouette, emphasizes it. Similarly, the dark-blue walls of the living room demonstrate how bright it is, thanks to three large sash windows. The colour also provides the perfect backdrop for Nina's growing art collection.

'I love art and would love to have more of it, but it is an expensive passion,' she says. 'I also collect small beautiful objects, travel mementos and fashion accessories. Somehow the mixture in the house just works. We are very happy here as a family, and that's what I love the most.'

ABOVE In the bedroom, walls painted in 'Setting Plaster' by Farrow & Ball provide a soothing backdrop to an 18th-century French bed. The bedside cabinet is from Nicky Haslam and the painting is by British artist Maya Hewitt.

OPPOSITE Of the dressing room, Nina says, 'I needed somewhere to put my shoes and came up with the idea of having the shelves at different heights. That makes it much easier when deciding what to wear.'

MORE IS MORE
TONY DUQUETTE

The Big Penis Book JIAN HANSON

ROBERT LONGO — CHARCOAL

CAROLINE LEGRAND

INTERIOR DESIGNER

'It hadn't been touched for 30 years, but straightaway I could see what I would do with it,' says Caroline Legrand of her Holland Park flat. It was relatively affordable for the area, but had languished on the market for some time, owing to the dated decor and awkward layout.

Ironically, Caroline's vision involved transforming the apartment with an in-your-face neo-1970s makeover, taking the best of the era and giving it a contemporary spin.

'People have the impression that the decade wasn't stylish, but the interiors were amazing,' she says. 'I love vintage furniture from the era, especially pieces that were made in limited editions by American designers. The quality is exceptional, and it's nice to buy things that aren't new and made in a factory.'

There's nothing cookie-cutter about this interior, as evidenced by the darkly glamorous sitting room with its chocolate-brown walls and parquet flooring. Rather than trying to make the north-facing room feel lighter by whitewashing it, Caroline has made a virtue of the gloomy aspect, turning what was cold into something cosy, even sexy.

'I want people to walk in and feel that they are being embraced,' she says. 'The room is dark regardless, so why try to make it light? It's important to respect the building. If you go against it, it's not going to work.'

Caroline bought the spectacular 1960s sectional sofa from vintage gallery Talisman. 'It was white, but the shape was perfect,' she recalls. 'I wanted something velvet in a warm colour.' The result is a caramel-gold

ABOVE LEFT AND OPPOSITE Simple seagrass walls provide a foil for the many statement pieces in the dining room, including a rug commissioned from Christopher Farr. Velvet dining chairs and curtains add another textural touch.

ABOVE RIGHT The leopard-print armchair – one of many retro pieces bought in Palm Springs – is complemented by the chocolate-brown walls of the living room.

upholstery fabric that adds to the louche atmosphere of the room, as do the ovoid Rougier lights and Lucite and travertine coffee table. Flashes of animal prints recall the retro interiors of such legendary decorators as Tony Duquette. This is a grown-up space for entertaining.

The adjoining dining room is bolder still. A 1970s bronze ram's-head table is teamed with vintage Lucite dining chairs and a newly commissioned Christopher Farr silk rug. Seagrass wallpaper adds textural depth.

Caroline has ensured that the hallway is as dramatic as the dark living spaces beyond. The marble-floored generous space has a gallery-like feel and houses most of her impressive art collection, with works by Ryan McGinley and Anish Kapoor, as well as more personal pieces by her two young sons.

'I've always said that a hallway is like your business card. It's often an afterthought that nobody bothers to decorate. But it's the first thing that you need to decorate. If you put a lot of energy into a hallway, it kind of carries through a house. People love it. They always say, "Wow, this is amazing!"'

What better first impression can an interior designer hope to make?

ABOVE LEFT Caroline professes a love of 1960s and '70s vintage and has several iconic designs, including this 'Hand' chair by Pedro Friedeberg.

ABOVE RIGHT AND OPPOSITE Of the pink walls in the kitchen, she says: 'I based the scheme around a photograph I bought from Frieze and matched the colour of the walls to the model's skin tone. It took about 10 tries to get the perfect pink.'

THIS PAGE Eye-catching design details abound, from bold upholstery fabrics (a Louis XIV-style chair in the master bathroom is upholstered in 'Leo' from Pierre Frey) to statement lamps and Lucite furniture. Even everyday objects, such as this cluster of perfume bottles and crystals, have been elevated to elegant vignettes.

OPPOSITE Caroline can't bring herself to part with the fabulously decadent throw in her glamorous bedroom. 'Being a vegetarian, I had got rid of all my furs, but this is the last one,' she says. 'It's going to have to go sooner or later.'

'People have an impression that the 1970s weren't stylish, but it was the best era: the people, the jet-set lifestyle, the amazing interiors.'

ALEX EAGLE

CREATIVE DIRECTOR

Shearling-covered sofas, vivid silk-cashmere throws, brass trays bearing the finest Venetian glassware – these are a few of the many luxe touches in the Soho home that fashion stylist-turned-retail mogul Alex Eagle shares with her husband, gallerist Mark Wadhwa.

But this is no glitzy, high-glam home – for although Alex's home is filled with fine furniture and art, it feels very open. The interior space stretches over 400 m² (4,300 sq ft), and Alex is attuned to making visitors feel at ease, even when most of us would baulk at the prospect of entertaining.

'We moved in on Christmas Eve and had 20 people over for lunch the next day,' she recalls. 'It was hectic but brilliant fun, and fortunately Mark already owned this table.'

The dining table in question comfortably seats 25, and can be extended to fit up to 35. The couple often bring another table out of storage to accommodate even more guests. 'For the Frieze Art Fair 2014, I hosted a dinner to celebrate Tanya Ling's show,' Alex says. 'We managed to fit in 65 people. It was a Monday evening, so we thought we'd get a lot of drop-outs, but everyone showed up.'

Until recently the table was also HQ for Alex's team, while she launched her eponymous shops. As well as a townhouse in Knightsbridge, there is a vast space at Soho House Berlin, another on Lexington Street (a short stroll from Alex's flat) and a store at cool country hangout Soho Farmhouse in Gloucestershire, all of which offer the beautifully curated mix of design, art and fashion evident in her own home.

ABOVE LEFT AND RIGHT The huge houseplants are meant to echo the leafy streets near Alex's childhood home in Chiswick. In the living area, the bookshelves were designed by Fran Hickman and built especially for the flat, while the little blue car is a vintage find.

OPPOSITE The sofa and armchair were bought in Paris, and the artwork is by photographer and filmmaker Alex Prager. The rattan chairs are a Charlotte Perriand design.

'It's nice to be able to try things out at home and I often sell things from the loft,' she says. 'There are very few walls here, so it feels like a stage set. Everything can be moved around quite easily.'

Anchoring the centre of the space, the bespoke Plain English kitchen creates a boundary between the open-plan dining and lounging area of one side, and a private zone with bedroom and bathrooms, a more formal sitting area and Alex's home office, where ceiling-height bookshelves run the length of the wall. Elsewhere, large-scale photographs and colourful sculptures add pops of interest.

Alex, who studied history of art before working as a fashion stylist for *Harper's Bazaar*, favours pieces by emerging talents, mixed with photographs by the likes of Guy Bourdin, Helmut Newton and Irving Penn, which are 'still comparatively affordable'.

Her appreciation of art was honed by her father, an art dealer, and her love of design by her mother, a 'serial decorator', who took Alex on regular trips to the antiques shops on Lots Road as a child. Huge cacti and figs echo the leafy streets near her childhood home in Chiswick, and compensate for the fact that the loft has no outdoor space.

'I love having greenery inside, especially when living in the centre of London – it's important to bring the outside in,' Alex says. 'It's my little oasis in the city.'

ABOVE AND OPPOSITE The kitchen, Alex says, 'was an investment, but it will last forever and acts as an anchor to the whole loft. The aesthetic is simple, spare and beautiful.'

ABOVE LEFT The multi-coloured pots on top of the antique French console are by Tortus Copenhagen. Above it is an abstract artwork by French artist Noémie Goudal.

RIGHT The desk and chair are vintage 1930s pieces and are available from Alex's store. Of the plant, she says, 'cacti are so old and somehow wise. They have such character.'

OPPOSITE The bed is upholstered in fabric from Pierre Frey; above it is a photograph by Olivo Barbieri. The table is vintage and the lamp is by Castor.

'Contemporary art
can be so expensive
and alienating.
I prefer art that
makes people feel
good and that they
find beautiful.'

JESSICA McCORMACK

JEWELRY DESIGNER

'I have a possession obsession, and for that you need big rooms,' says New Zealand-born Jessica McCormack. 'I'm a big believer in going with your gut. Don't worry about themes: mix different styles and eras that reflect your personality. Surround yourself with what makes you happy.'

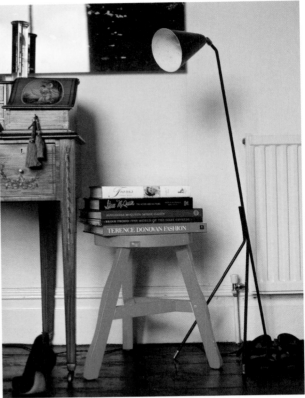

'Glam gothic' is how Jessica describes her showstopping jewelry designs, and it is also the perfect way to describe how she has decorated her home in Notting Hill. Darkly glamorous and filled with art, antiques and contemporary design, it's exactly the kind of place that her clients (Rihanna and Madonna, among them) would feel right at home.

Jessica's talent for creating surprising combinations means that the eclectic furnishings sit together comfortably in the large Victorian home she shares with her husband Douglas and their son. The high-ceilinged rooms with white walls and dark floors are ideal for displaying her favourite finds. Old Master paintings and carved Bavarian chairs are mixed with modern designs by Studio Job, along with everything from monkey skulls to pickled hearts – motifs that she also uses in her jewels.

'My look is about adding an urban contemporary edge to traditional pieces,' she explains. 'I like to mix the clean lines of Zaha Hadid with over-the-top taxidermy and old paintings.'

The living room houses some impressive artworks, including a sculpture by New York-based Huma Bhabha, a charcoal piece by the American painter and sculptor Robert Longo and a photograph by Louise Lawler. The

ABOVE LEFT AND RIGHT The living room contains several works of art and other, more eccentric pieces, including this skull. The orange stool is a Tom Dixon design.

OPPOSITE A salvaged shipping light hangs above a dining table by B&B Italia. Behind it is a photograph by Dionisio González.

'I love the juxtaposition of this feminine desk with the Anne Hardy artwork. The chair reminds me of a quilted Chanel bag.'

sleek, white coffee table by Barber & Osgerby for Established & Sons provides a visual counterpoint to a fluorescent orange stool by Tom Dixon and vintage Persian carpets.

And in the hallway is a striking work by New York-based artist Marilyn Minter. 'She paints on photographs and is one of my favourite artists at the moment,' Jessica says. 'I'm intrigued by the jewel-like quality of this piece.'

But how does a small child fit into this artfully curated space that's full of fragile, valuable things? 'I am under no illusion,' Jessica admits. 'At some stage, my son will turn into a wrecking ball. But in the same way that I think you should always wear your jewels so they are appreciated and loved, the same goes for art. If we saved everything wonderful for special or non-child occasions, life would be very dull, indeed.'

Jessica's own childhood in New Zealand was anything but dull; she grew up surrounded by 'eccentric, crazy old stuff' brought home by her father, an antiques dealer and auctioneer.

'I learned to appreciate quality and things with history early on,' she says. 'It also gave me a taste for seeing things in one context and giving them a new lease of life. When you put things in an unexpected environment, they take on a new dimension.'

ABOVE A work by British artist Walead Beshty hangs above the bed. The lamp on the vintage side table (with faux books) is from Simon James Design.

OPPOSITE Stone adzes from Papua New Guinea sit on the mantelpiece in the dressing room. In the bedroom is a carved 17th-century chair.

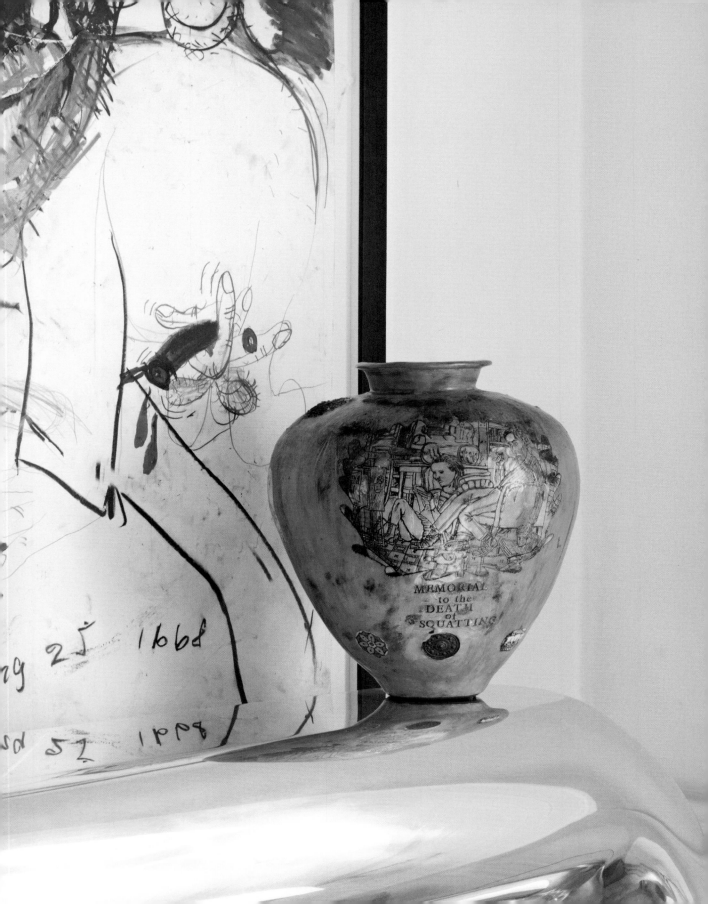

MEMORIAL
to the
DEATH
of
SQUATTING

FRANCIS SULTANA

Designer Francis Sultana is commissioned by some of the most influential – and affluent – people in the world. The Piccadilly apartment he shares with his partner, the gallerist David Gill, is full of art, and the couple have found a niche filling clients' houses with art and design.

Far from being an afterthought, however, the art comes first and if a client loves something – a canvas, a sculpture, a table – Francis will 'find a way to make it work'. He doesn't peddle bland, beige interiors, and ensures that his clients are surrounded by the extraordinary every day.

Francis lives in the Albany, a prestigious set of apartments tucked behind the Royal Academy of Art. Originally built for bachelors in the 1770s, famous residents have included William Gladstone and Lord Byron, and numerous members of the aristocracy. 'I like the location, the architecture and its history,' he says. 'But I was also fascinated by David Hicks from the age of eight. He lived here, and so I wanted to live here, too.'

Born on the Maltese island of Gozo, Francis moved to London aged 19 and found work at Gill's gallery, of which he is now

CEO, where he honed his knowledge about design and art. He now has his own line of bespoke furniture, several pieces of which are in his home.

The couple's eclectic collection of contemporary art and design includes pots by Grayson Perry, works by Jake and Dinos Chapman (including a naked figure in a bell jar with a penis for a nose and an anus for a mouth) and slick, glossy shelving by the late Zaha Hadid. A favourite piece is a chair by Emilio Terry, which originally sat in the

ABOVE LEFT A vase designed by Grayson Perry in the dining room. 'I knew him years ago and used to sell his work at the gallery,' says Francis.

OPPOSITE The living room features a Garouste & Bonetti coffee table. A sculptural black 'King Bonk' chair is positioned beside a shelf by Zaha Hadid and an abstract painting by the artist Christopher Wool.

'Our home is a space
that reflects the
things we love and
have meaning to
our life together.'

Le Corbusier-designed penthouse on the Champs-Élysées.

Somehow, Francis has created a stylish, harmonious whole in this most traditional of settings. 'Ultimately, it's the fusion that makes my style work,' he says. 'I love commissioning other artists to create pieces for my projects – creating a language that evokes the personality of my clients. Our home is a space that is about reflecting the things we love and have meaning to our life together.'

Despite being surrounded by so many beautiful and important pieces, Francis claims that the apartment is 'the most un-interior designed place I've ever done', and that practicality and comfort were the overriding considerations. Nor is he precious about furnishings: the book-

lined study has the worn elegance of a country house, with the frayed sofas merely adding to the charm.

Home comforts feature prominently on his list of priorities – 'exceptional bedlinen and towels, scented candles, cashmere throws' – and he is happiest cooking a roast chicken on a winter's evening.

'Having delicious food to cook and good friends to share it with is my idea of a perfect weekend,' Francis says. And the Chapman brothers' figurine is guaranteed to be a conversation-starter.

ABOVE LEFT AND RIGHT In the study are sofas by Eugène Printz that the couple have had for 25 years. An elegant console doubles as a desk.

OPPOSITE Framed original artworks from classic comic books add a lighthearted touch in the master bedroom.

MATILDA GOAD

STYLIST

Matilda Goad is a young woman with an old soul. On a mission to make people appreciate the 'old-fashioned, simple pleasures of life', her charming line of home accessories, from scalloped raffia lampshades to framed botanical prints, have been a hit with the fashion crowd.

Matilda uses the bijoux Notting Hill flat she shares with her husband Tom as a testing ground for new ideas and as a backdrop for shoots. It might be small, but the interior is perfectly formed, with plenty of decorating ideas to steal.

'The apartment block was pretty rundown,' she says. 'But from the moment I saw the 1930s architecture and Crittall windows, it felt very special, especially when shiny new developments are going up all over London.'

When the couple moved in they pulled up carpets, painted the floorboards white, and added colour to the walls and a few seagrass rugs to make the place feel cosier. Matilda buys antique and mid-century furniture at nearby Portobello market, having no qualms about mixing different styles in a small space. She is equally brave in her colour choices.

'There's a spot in the flat where you look past the dark walls and black door frame into my pink-walled bedroom with a delicate lamp sitting on an old French table,' she says. 'That's what makes me excited.'

In the sitting room, a pair of orange velvet armchairs sit against deep-green walls, the flatness of the colour contrasting beautifully with the sheen of the velvet. The space is

ABOVE LEFT AND RIGHT The façade of the 1930s apartment block features distinctive Crittall windows. Fresh flowers are a 'necessary extravagance'.

OPPOSITE The dining area is painted a sludgy green. 'In a small, north-facing flat, dark-green walls wouldn't normally be a traditional choice,' Matilda notes. 'But the ceiling is quite high, which makes the room feel cosy, yet still spacious.'

dominated by a giant antique mirror above the mantel, which Matilda bought on her first date with Tom at Petersham Nurseries. 'It got dropped during delivery and the mercury film started to peel in the heat, but that just adds to the charm for me,' she says. 'It almost feels like painting in the room.'

The bedroom is an airy and serene space, with a grey cane bed frame and Hungarian linen curtains with a faint pink line that exactly matches the colour of the walls. Matilda is big on small, elegant touches, citing flowers as her greatest extravagance. 'I have a huge collection of vases,' she admits, 'and in a flat starved of storage space, that's definitely an indulgence.'

Despite the fact that the kitchen is 'tiny', the couple are prodigious hosts, with Tom regularly whipping up dinner for up to

14 guests, while Matilda creates an elegant mise-en-scène. 'I love making the atmosphere feel special,' she says. 'Whether we have friends over or not, playing music in the background and using our favourite glasses always lifts the mood. For the dinner table, using oyster shells as salt and pepper cellars, beautiful candles and crisp linen feels like such a luxury at the end of a long day.'

ABOVE AND OPPOSITE The bedroom is a feminine space with pale-pink walls and scalloped lampshades, as well as a serene spot for sketching new designs. On the bedside table is Matilda's collection of crystals.

LEE BROOM

INTERIOR DESIGNER

Lee Broom, a former child actor, is now known
for designing commercial interiors that are
sophisticated yet playful. This experience has
informed the look of his sleek and spectacular flat,
located on the ground floor and basement of
a converted Victorian fire station in Kennington.

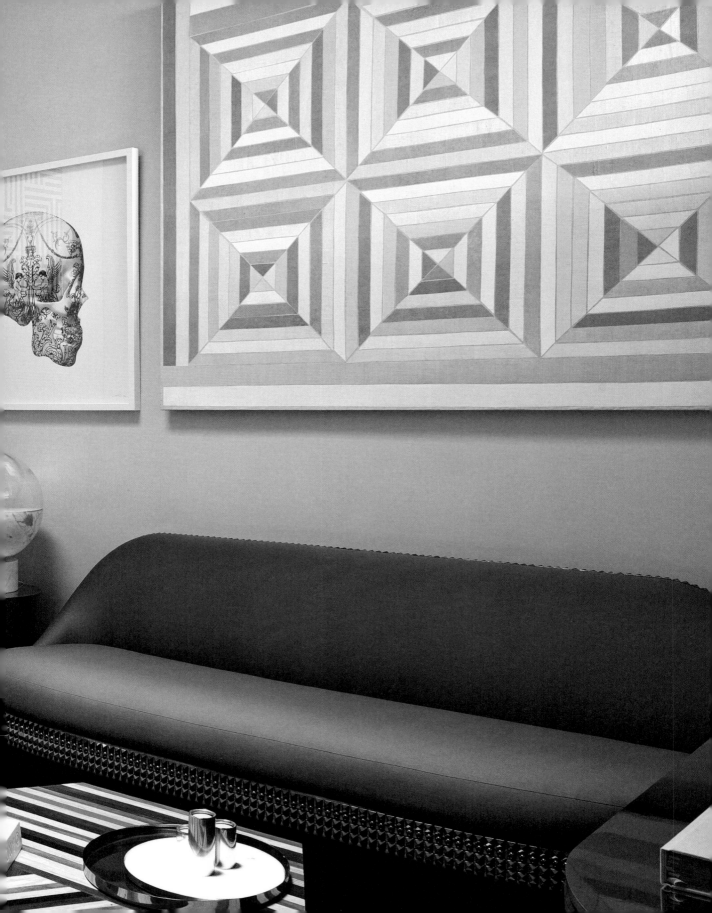

Immediately upon entering there is an airy atrium, with a soaring ceiling from which a gold hoop chair is suspended. It is one of several of Lee's glamorous designs that fill the space; others include a striped 'Parquetry' coffee table and a studded 'Salon' sofa. A work by the textile artist Serena Wells, together with the books, sculptures and lamps on plinths, add to the gallery-like feel.

Lee and his partner Charles Rudgard have significantly renovated the flat, removing walls and exposing steel girders to create an open-plan, loft-like layout on the ground floor. Dark wood floors and 'pebble'-coloured walls and ceilings reflect Lee's signature look, which he describes as 'luxurious but with an edge, like combining Mayfair with East London. It's fun but formal at the same time.'

The basement level is definitely the fun part of this home. As well as two bedrooms, there's an entirely mirrored downstairs loo and a red-walled cinema room, added after a cavity filled with 15 tons of building rubble was discovered and repurposed.

'We hadn't bargained on the space, so we felt that we could do something different with it,' says Lee. 'A home needs to have some elements of fun and playfulness. This flat reflects all the different bits of my personality.'

ABOVE AND OPPOSITE The open-plan kitchen-diner features a plush banquette with integrated lighting, a nod to Lee's experience designing restaurants and bars. The cluster of lights above the kitchen island is his own design, and adds decoration to the otherwise sleek kitchen, which Lee, who doesn't cook, insists is kept clutter-free.

'I approached my home the way I would a commercial project. There needs to be a sense of drama and an emotional connection as soon as you walk in.'

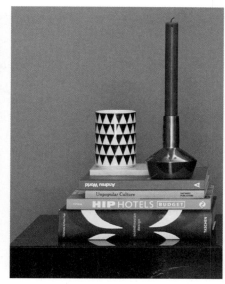

THIS PAGE An oversized German railway clock in the kitchen; the 'Split' mirror and 'Carpetry' console are two of Lee's own designs, as is the cluster of 'Chamber' pendant lights. A carpet-clad sideboard in the living room is typical of Lee's playful designs. The biker jacket that hangs in the hallway once belonged to the artist Keith Haring and is one of Lee's most prized possessions.

HUBERT ZANDBERG

COLLECTOR AND INTERIOR DESIGNER

In an era when shedding possessions is fashionable and interior architecture is championed over decoration, designer Hubert Zandberg's intoxicatingly maximalist work has been known to convert even the staunchest minimalists to the power of beautiful objects.

In Hubert's five-storey Ladbroke Grove home, every surface – even doors and ceilings – is decorated with art, artefacts and an extraordinary array of curios. His collection is carefully curated, so that the house becomes a living museum to be explored. Visitors enter the sitting room straight from the street, and are immediately enveloped by the 'more is more' decorating philosophy.

'I was looking for a space that could house the collection, and decorating this place gave me the perfect opportunity to experiment,' Hubert says. 'The layout is higgledy-piggledy and stylistically it's nothing special, but it became a laboratory of ideas. I thought I may as well have fun, and each room ultimately became a sort of cabinet of curiosities.'

The house was originally a canal-keeper's house on the Grand Union Canal, the basement storing hay, horses and coaches;

later it became a sweet shop and then a motorcycle repair shop. Some rooms have low ceilings, while others soar, and there are undulating curves, unexpected rooms and architectural oddities, including the old shop windows at street level.

To 'lose' the tricky architecture in the sitting room, Hubert painted the walls chocolate brown and the ceiling black before layering in his hugely varied collection.

ABOVE Seashells on top of one of Hubert's many carefully curated cabinets of curiosities.

OPPOSITE In the sitting room, chocolate-brown walls provide a rich backdrop against which all manner of curios – from prehistoric tusks to contemporary photography – are displayed.

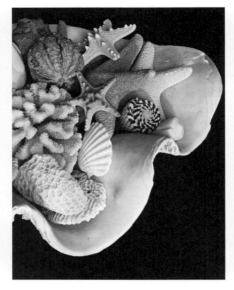

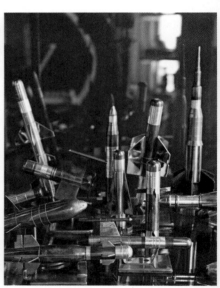

THIS PAGE 'People generally love it,' Hubert says of the decoration. 'It encourages exploration and conversation.' But there is one pedestrian question that he abhors: 'I hate it when people ask how I keep things clean.' The answer? 'I don't – I have a cleaner who enjoys dusting. I think it's easier to clean a house like this than one with five kids, endless dishes and a greasy oven.'

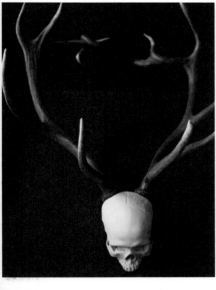

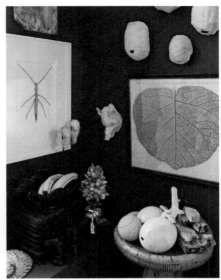

THIS PAGE Hubert's fearless more-is-more approach to interior decoration is intoxicatingly seductive, and the very antithesis of the current fashion for clutter-free living and streamlined architecture.

'I wanted it to look like it was mounted on infinity, so that there was absolutely nothing to distract from the objects and the art,' Hubert explains. 'It became an exercise in combining pieces, and a bit of a challenge to see how many things I could put together without the balance being off.'

Hundreds, if not thousands, of objects fill every room of the house, even the bathroom and basement kitchen. There are prehistoric artefacts, including a mammoth tusk, wall-mounted tortoiseshells, contemporary photography, a Zulu skirt that is a nod to Hubert's childhood in South Africa, vintage Italian furniture … the inventory could go on and on. A tonal colour palette and the fact that many of the items relate to nature helps to ensure the atmosphere is quiet, rather than chaotic, encouraging hushed admiration.

'For me, it's actually very calming, weirdly, because it's so deeply personal,' says Hubert. 'It's all about me and the pieces I decided to bring in. They're never really yours – you just take care of them for a time.'

ABOVE RIGHT Even the study has colourful art, statement lighting and a taxidermy flamingo for good measure. Patchworks of rugs in many of the rooms almost create the effect of wall-to-wall carpet.

OPPOSITE In the dressing room, old luggage racks from French trains serve as shelves and passementerie from a very old Parisian shop is draped over the top of hangers to keep dust off coats and jackets. The walls are painted in 'Skylight' by Farrow & Ball.

THIS PAGE The black-and-white bathroom is crammed with monochrome collections, including a shelf of environmentally farmed coral. The framed photographs include male nudes by George Dureau (Robert Mapplethorpe's mentor), a gift from the artist. There are also prints of newspaper reportage from the 1930s and '40s. 'Framing black-and-white images is a cheap way to create impact – some of these are just Getty images,' Hubert says.

LAURA MYERS

FASHION DESIGNER

Having grown up in Auckland, New Zealand, fashion designer Laura Myers has brought the laid-back spirit of the South Pacific to buttoned-up Belgravia, and her home has a light, bright vibe that is more in keeping with antipodean style than with overstuffed English interiors.

'Whenever I come home I always feel so calm,' says Laura of the handsome townhouse. 'The bones of the place are British, but the feeling isn't fussy or strict. A relaxed attitude is definitely part of the Kiwi approach to life. I wanted the house to feel very serene and have an easy flow from room to room.'

She bought the three-storey Georgian property four years ago and gave it a 'largely cosmetic' overhaul by painting everything white, installing new flooring and adding smart hardware such as light switches and door handles. The biggest change was in the kitchen, which has been reconfigured and freshened up with new cabinets.

The neutral backdrop has been layered with artfully composed collections of objects: carved Maori walking sticks in the living room, works by New Zealand photographer Derek Henderson in the kitchen, coconut fibre fans from the Cook Islands in the living room and Samoan wallhangings in the guest bedroom. All manner of seashells are dotted throughout the house.

'I wanted to surround myself with things that felt like home and collected quite a lot of pieces from around the South Pacific,' Laura says. 'I really like that island sort of feeling.'

ABOVE LEFT AND RIGHT Laura wears a design from her label, Atea Oceanie. Carved Maori walking sticks, propped against the living-room wall, are one of many touches from the South Pacific islands.

OPPOSITE On the first floor, a light-suffused formal dining area has French doors that open out to a terrace. A seashell mirror hangs above the mantel.

Her fashion label Atea Oceanie was inspired by the need for an effortless capsule wardrobe while travelling. The relaxed designs have won a legion of high-profile fans: Kate Moss, Sarah Jessica Parker and Poppy Delevingne have all been spotted in Laura's designs.

In the basement bedroom, tall Art Deco-style chests of drawers and curtains made from vintage Greek tablecloths add an elegant touch. Double doors lead out to a lushly planted courtyard garden, where a studio apartment is decorated like the ultimate pool house. 'If only the weather was warm enough for a pool!' Laura says, jovially.

On the light-suffused first floor, a huge seashell-framed mirror sits on the mantelpiece in a more formal dining area with a 1960s table and Lucite chairs. Next door, a high-ceilinged drawing room with intricate plaster mouldings has the look of a grand ballroom in miniature. The pale palette allows the architecture to sing and individual details come to the fore, such as a lustrous inlaid mother-of-pearl tabletop.

ABOVE LEFT AND RIGHT A cool – and kitsch – collection of vintage finds 'from here, there and everywhere' in the first-floor dining area.

OPPOSITE Framed Samoan tapa cloth adds a hit of pattern in the elegant drawing room. Metal wall lights and a Jieldé floor lamp add an industrial touch.

The table was a gift from Laura's mother, the Auckland-based interior designer Stephanie Overton, who helped with the decoration. 'I've always loved interiors, thanks to my mother,' Laura says. 'One of our favourite things to do together is moving furniture around and rearranging the rooms. It keeps the house alive.'

ABOVE LEFT AND RIGHT The all-white master bedroom in the basement, with its hotel-inspired en suite, is surprisingly bright and has views of the courtyard garden, which also has a summerhouse that doubles as a spare bedroom.

OPPOSITE Laura has created the illusion of space in the cosy guest bedroom by mirroring one wall. Tucked beneath the eaves on one side is a bathroom and on the other is a small but perfectly formed kitchen.

CLEMENTS RIBEIRO

FASHION DESIGNERS

Suzanne Clements and Inacio Ribeiro's eye for craft and quality is reflected in the eccentric yet elegant home they share with their family in Bayswater. The five-bedroom house dates back to 1850, but when they bought it in 2005 the period charm had been obscured by decades of decay.

'While we're enjoying the house looking so minimal, we love a mad, busy home. This is the calm before the storm!'

Having met on their first day as students at Central St Martins, marriage and a business soon followed – although, as Inacio says, 'we're different in background, temperament and taste'. This creative counterbalance led to commercial success: their label's eclectic, feminine style shaped the late 1990s London fashion scene, and its colourful, witty sweaters made Scottish cashmere cool.

'Our aesthetic was always a melting pot of the two of us,' says Suzanne. Of the house, she adds: 'We left it quite scruffy and undone for the first seven years, before we finally got round to the dreaded renovations. The house basically needed a complete restoration.'

The cost of the build meant there wasn't much money left over for furniture, so except for beds and a couple of mid-century pieces, everything else has come from 'junk shops, skips or hand-me-downs'.

Although the house has been sparsely furnished, the skilful use of colour ensures that it is still characterful. Strikingly, each of the five floors of the stairwell has been painted in a different shade of green. 'I wanted to avoid white rooms at all costs,' Suzanne explains. 'I prefer moody colours, as they're so much more atmospheric.'

The ground-floor sitting room is jade green and the adjoining office is a deep navy. Up a floor, the family room is a sludgy green-brown (Farrow & Ball's 'Drab 41', an archive colour), as is the master bedroom. Blue and

ABOVE RIGHT The navy-walled ground-floor study, next door to the sitting room.

OPPOSITE The jade sitting room sets the tone for the blue-green colour palette that runs through the house, getting gradually lighter on the upper floors.

black walls in the bathrooms are covered with photos, and Suzanne's dressing room is a delicious shade of peach. The exception is the kitchen in the light-starved basement, which does feature lots of white.

After reviving the fortunes of Cacharel during a stint as creative directors of the French fashion house in the 2000s, in 2007 the couple decided to focus on diversifying their own label. Inacio now consults for fashion brands in Italy, spending much of his time there, and Suzanne focuses on their line of wallpaper and furnishing fabrics for the American interiors company, Schumacher.

Many of the paintings and sculptures on display have been collected by the couple during travels to Brazil over the years. There are also unusual and evocative objects from Inacio's homeland, including a ceremonial headdress from an Amazonian tribe. These

will soon be joined by other flashes of decoration, as Suzanne is planning on putting up some of their wallpaper designs and, surprisingly, adding in some clutter.

'We completely stripped back during the renovations and the clutter hasn't crept back in yet,' she says. 'I have been overly precious about banging nails in the walls and hanging paintings. But while I'm enjoying the house looking so minimal, I love a mad, busy home. This is the calm before the storm!'

ABOVE LEFT AND OPPOSITE The master bedroom is a calm, uncluttered space, which blends traditional details such as the built-in wardrobe doors with contemporary styling.

ABOVE RIGHT Graphic floor tiles from Fired Earth and a clawfoot bathtub add interest in the en-suite bathroom.

BASSO & BROOKE

FASHION DESIGNERS

Britain excels at producing exciting print designers, but few have had such eye-popping impact as Bruno Basso and Christopher Brooke. Like their print designs, their own home is glossy, cartoon-bright and visually hyperactive, and acts as a living canvas.

After bursting onto the fashion scene in 2003, their prints have been worn by the likes of Katy Perry and Michelle Obama, making the couple among the first UK designers to be worn by the former First Lady.

'When we started out, digital printing was still in its infancy,' says Christopher. 'We won the first Fashion Fringe competition in 2004, and pretty much pioneered the digital-print process in the fashion industry.'

Since then he and Bruno have splashed kaleidoscopic patterns across wallpaper, cushions, tableware, and more. Unlike perfumers who prefer not to wear scent or fashion designers who dress only in black, this duo practise what they preach when it comes to design decisions for their own home.

Classic French furniture has been given a zingy update with the application of neon paint and patchwork prints, pieced together

like digital découpage. Their work is highly technical and complex, but it is also playful, with irreverent motifs hidden in the frenetic patterns. Cartoonish touches are also dotted about the flat; Mickey Mouse posters, pop-art bunnies, model dinosaurs and wooden clown puppets all make an appearance. There are more smirk-inducing objects, too, including phallic vases by Ettore Sottsass (whose motto – 'You don't save your soul just painting everything white' – they also subscribe to).

ABOVE LEFT AND RIGHT The sitting room features a eclectic mix of furnishing in electric hues. Even the hearth has been given a digitally printed makeover.

OPPOSITE A vivid wall mural designed by the couple, French-style armchair and Habitat floor lamp, topped with one of the duo's shades.

'When we started out, digital printing was still in its infancy, and we ran with it.'

The couple may have turned their attention to interiors, but the result is dynamic, vibrant and whimsical – the opposite of matchy-matchy fabrics aimed at the masses. 'We have always been interested in interiors and think of our label as a lifestyle brand,' Bruno says.

In 2017 the duo launched Jupiter 10, producing wallpaper designs inspired by cities they have visited around the world. They also run the print-design consultancy Artwork Club, working with fashion houses, high-street stores and clients around the world.

When they met in a nightclub in the 1990s, Christopher was working as a stylist for pop acts including Kylie Minogue and Robbie Williams after studying fashion design, while Bruno was a graphic designer. They soon became work and life partners.

'We have worked together almost from the start of our relationship, so we haven't known any different,' says Bruno. 'We're both very driven and enjoy working, and sometimes we forget to switch off. We live to work.'

Clearly they live their work, too.

OPPOSITE An eye-popping patchwork of prints in the master bedroom.

THIS PAGE Kitsch and cartoonish objects are sprinkled throughout the space, from wooden puppets to phallic vases and Fornasetti urns.

CARINA COOPER

COOKERY WRITER

A self-confessed serial mover, Carina Cooper has lived in 'a couple of townhouses, a farmhouse, a Mediterranean *finca* and this little place, tucked away in a gated cobbled mews'. The secluded location of her Notting Hill home means that it doesn't feel like it's in the middle of the city.

'It's about positioning objects and appreciating them for their qualities. I love everything to count.'

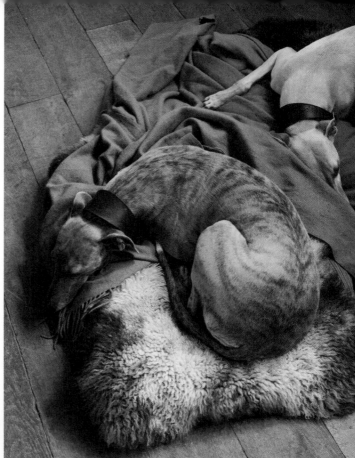

The house has a neighbourly, open-door vibe encouraged and nurtured by Carina, and weekends often have the convivial air of a street-party. 'My house is a drop-by home, and people tend to wander in and out all day,' she says.

'When the weather's fine, the doors are always open and look out to my neighbour's house, which is covered in glorious climbing roses and jasmine. I'll often throw a lunch for friends using fresh ingredients from the local farmers' market.'

Carina has written several recipe books, among them the bestselling *Notting Hill Cookbook*, which she wrote at the suggestion of her ex-husband, the film director Franc Roddam, who also created the format for the TV show *Masterchef*. But despite her love of

cooking, Carina has not installed a glossy, state-of-the-art kitchen in her home. Like the rest of the interior, the kitchen is rustic, low key and in keeping with the building's humble origins as stabling for horses.

'There is something special, a calmness, about living in a dwelling that originally housed animals,' she says. 'I do believe that walls hold energy, and that we pick up vibes in houses. I get a warm glow when people say they like the feeling of my house.'

ABOVE LEFT AND RIGHT A cloudscape by a 19th-century Russian painter reminds Carina of the summer skies in her holiday home of Ibiza. The family whippets Echo and Dash have a snooze on the floor.

OPPOSITE A vintage rattan rocker by the log-burner in the kitchen.

Carina talks about 'energy' a great deal and peppers her conversation with talk of sacred symbols and vibrations. Even cynical souls will be soothed by her gentle, calming presence and the atmosphere of her home, which she attributes to following the Japanese philosophy of *wabi-sabi*.

'It's about positioning objects and appreciating their qualities,' she says. 'William Morris's quote about only having beautiful or practical objects really resonates with me.' She adds that if she could change one thing about her home, it would be to add a Japanese wooden bathtub, which is most certainly both practical and beautiful, yet some of Carina's favourite items are purely decorative.

'My biggest extravagance is buying art,' she says. 'When I sold my last house, I said to my four daughters that they could each

choose an artwork, which I would invest in if I liked it. I was astounded by their choices, and that they all have blue in common.'

A cloudscape reminds Carina of summertime in Ibiza, where she has 'a small *ranchito*' surrounded by almond trees, which she intends to harvest and farm in years to come. For now, however, she is content with her small oasis of calm in the city.

ABOVE LEFT AND RIGHT The quirky stairwell has a Moroccan flavour, thanks to a fretwork panel and tin lantern. A cosy reading nook in the basement sitting room is Carina's favourite spot in the house.

OPPOSITE Carina's passion for Eastern mysticism is apparent in the wallhangings, books and Buddhas that are dotted about the place.

GILLIAN HYLAND

PHOTOGRAPHER AND STYLIST

Most people would rip out an orange Formica kitchen and replace it with something sleeker, but Gillian Hyland decided to put one in when she renovated her two-bedroom 1930s flat in Clapton. 'I'm really into colour, so I was very excited,' she says, 'but the builders thought I was mad.'

In another colour-confident move, Gillian offset cabinets with bright teal-blue walls, which carry through into the open-plan living area. Fishscale-patterned floor tiles in myriad blues and whites sweep from the kitchen down into the hallway and the bathroom beyond. It's safe to assume that Gillian is no decorating wallflower.

'I had a freestanding 1950s kitchen unit for years,' she says, 'with doors made from Formica, which has a vintage retro feel. It's a brilliant material, because it's very hardwearing, is wipeable and comes in a million colours. Whereas most people want a kitchen in an open-plan space to recede into the background, for me it was about how to make it pretty enough to be part of your living room.'

The strength of vision is equally bold here: vintage mid-century furniture sits alongside kitsch travel finds and contemporary lighting, including brass and opaline glass fittings by Michael Anastassiades.

'They were inspired by 1930s moon lights,' Gillian notes. 'A lot of high-street stuff has a characterful, vintage edge to it. I like an eclectic mix of things.'

ABOVE LEFT AND OPPOSITE The crewel-work curtains in the living room are from Anthropologie. 'I've had them for years,' Gillian says. 'Subconsciously I think they have influenced the colour scheme.'

ABOVE RIGHT Panelling makes the dining area feel more characterful. A concealed door hides a utility area: 'I've always loved secret doors and did research on Pinterest to get it right,' Gillian says.

Having worked in magazines and TV as a fashion stylist and set designer in her native Ireland before moving to London 11 years ago, Gillian is well practised in the art of conjuring dramatic sets. 'I just really like materials, colours and textures, whether in wardrobe or interiors,' she says. 'Clients like the fact that I can do all the set design and props, as well as the wardrobe: there's one person overseeing the whole look.'

Gillian also takes evocative art photographs based on her own poetry, which hang around the flat. They often depict isolated characters in emotional situations and have the air of classic film stills. 'It brings together every side of what I like to do,' she says. 'I'll plan them, find the locations, source the props and wardrobe, do the casting and take the pictures. I'll sit with the images in my head for ages before actually shooting.'

She took the same approach to revamping the flat, planning the revised layout and project-managing the six-month build herself. Although everything was replaced, the finished interior feels timeless, or rather out of time, like one of Gillian's photographs.

'They're both such personal projects – that's why I wanted to do everything myself,' she explains. 'Giving someone else control just didn't feel right.'

ABOVE RIGHT AND OPPOSITE The pressed-glass lampshades above the kitchen countertop have an old-fashioned brasserie feel and mirror the engineered glass fronts of the kitchen cabinets, which have been taken right up to the ceiling.

ABOVE LEFT The screenprinted wallpaper in the study is by British maker Hannah Nunn. 'I love it because it's contemporary, but has a nostalgic feel,' Gillian says.

ABOVE RIGHT The bathroom features metro tiles from Fired Earth – also in teal – and a traditional clawfoot bath.

OPPOSITE The glamorous master bedroom has a calmer colour palette, reminiscent of a Hollywood starlet's boudoir, with gold walls, silk bedding and a 1950s chandelier.

ADAM BROWN

FASHION DESIGNER

Adam Brown travels a lot. The whole premise of his resort label Orlebar Brown is providing colourful classic clothing for a seemingly endless summer. The sun is always shining somewhere in the world, and the company ensures that its well-heeled clientele is suitably attired.

For Adam, however, the constant travelling is more business than pleasure, and time spent at home – a beautiful stucco-fronted townhouse in the heart of Notting Hill – is all the more precious.

The three-bedroom property has classic Georgian proportions, but the ground and first floors have both been knocked into one room per floor (a kitchen-diner and sitting room, respectively) that are perfect for entertaining, which Adam and his partner, PR executive Tom Konig-Oppenheimer, do regularly.

The couple bought the property in 2013 and utterly transformed the formerly hard-edged interior, which was all black, white and tempered glass. 'It's completely different now,' says Adam. 'We ripped everything out and started again to make it feel warm and comfortable and masculine.'

To achieve this, Adam enlisted the talents of interior designer Jonathan Reed, who he describes as a 'genius', with 'the most amazing eye for colour, materials, comfort and style'. Adam and Tom are in good company; Jonathan's clients have included David Bowie and Iman, and Elle Macpherson. Before founding his design practice, he worked at Hackett and Polo Ralph Lauren, creating interiors that mined the heritage of

ABOVE LEFT AND RIGHT A black-and-white palette, enlivened by strong splashes of primary colours, runs across the ground floor, creating a masculine look. Contrasting textures – wood, lacquer, brushed suede – add depth and tactility.

OPPOSITE Custom seating and Crittall-style partitions help to make a snug reception room appear more spacious.

the quintessential gentleman's club, and this tasteful, wood-panelled vibe is apparent at the Brown-Konig-Oppenheimer residence.

'We wanted a home that gets better with age and won't date,' Adam explains. 'I prefer natural finishes with lots of colour but muted, earthy tones. That said, I don't like anything too taupe or matchy-matchy.'

The upshot is a timeless home with bursts of modernity, peppered with a handful of just-off-the-catwalk looks. Many of the furnishings are bespoke designs by Jonathan, and provide a tastefully muted base against which bolder pieces ping, including a Grayson Perry artwork that hangs above the sofa in the sitting room.

The elegant yet masculine kitchen is Adam's favourite room in the house, although he admits to having a full-time housekeeper

and rarely has time to cook. His most treasured memories of home are movie nights in with the dogs and drinks with friends on the terrace, all of which sounds idyllic. But is there anything that he would change about his stylish slice of prime London real estate?

'I'd move it to north Cornwall, overlooking the beach!' he laughs. It seems the grass really is always greener ...

ABOVE AND OPPOSITE Pops of yellow and blue add a jolly dash of colour to the airy dining room. The 'Grasshopper' floor lamp is from Gubi.

ABOVE LEFT A time-worn leather armchair provides the perfect perch for a pooch.

OPPOSITE The master bedroom has a stylish and practical statement headboard with adjustable reading lamps. In place of traditional bedside cabinets, floating shelves help to free up floor space.

MATTHEW WILLIAMSON

FASHION DESIGNER

Even the most committed minimalist couldn't help but smile on entering Matthew Williamson's flat. The vivid pink of the hallway casts a rosy glow and provides a backdrop to floral garlands and gilt mirrors. It also hints at what's to come in this two-bedroom home in northwest London.

This fashion designer doesn't do neutrals; there are bursts of rainbow colours in every room. The grandly proportioned sitting and dining room, for example, has a bay of windows with canary yellow frames, a capacious turquoise velvet sofa and a chimney breast covered with parrot-print wallpaper.

'I would call my look organized bohemia,' he says. 'People laugh at me because I have all these vintage pieces and knickknacks around me at home, but my cushions have to be in the right place. They're currently not and that's driving me crazy. I like there to be a sense of order.'

While Matthew admits his home is 'done', there is nonetheless a random, effortless quality to it. Much like his design signature, it draws on the lure of far-flung lands and the louche glamour of the jet set in decades gone by.

'I was born in Manchester, which was quite cold and grey, so going to places like India and Brazil was creatively energizing,' he explains. 'The culture became part of the DNA of my look, along with my mum's approach to fashion and meeting Jade Jagger.'

Jagger, along with Kate Moss and Helena Christensen, memorably modelled jewel-coloured dresses from Matthew's first

ABOVE LEFT AND OPPOSITE The parrot wallpaper on the chimney breast is one of Matthew's own designs for Osborne & Little.

ABOVE RIGHT Matthew's upscale boho look is actually a mix of high style and lo-fi DIY; the fringed lampshades, for example, he made himself by customizing high-street shades.

collection in 1997. The show lasted just seven minutes and featured 11 outfits, but was enough to catapult the label to global success. Matthew's bohemian style has changed little since – unusual in an industry that demands something new every six months.

All around his home are hits of colour and pattern. The furniture is eye-catching and eclectic, covered in kaleidoscopic prints, including Matthew's signature butterfly motifs. Many of the pieces are his own designs (he has designed for Osborne & Little and Debenhams) or DIY revamps, from a lampshade updated with boho fringing to brightly painted dining chairs.

While the 'scale and great bones' of the building attracted him to the flat, Matthew has also radically revamped the layout, removing an en suite to make the master bedroom bigger and taking part of the formerly 'huge' kitchen to add a second

bedroom and shower room. The new galley kitchen has white units and walls, but isn't short on personality. Cobalt-blue pendants add a kick of colour, and even in this functional space Matthew shows his knack for displaying vintage finds en masse.

Matthew's home boldly and beautifully shows that style isn't about conforming to fads or following others. It's about expressing yourself and celebrating what inspires you.

ABOVE LEFT Further examples of Matthew's irreverent upcycling are evident in the living room, where a floral oil painting has been refreshed with a teal background.

ABOVE RIGHT In the hallway, a peacock rattan chair has been painted to match the intense colours of the hallway.

OPPOSITE Colourful ceramics in the all-white galley kitchen, and a pouffe covered in one of Matthew's fabrics for Osborne & Little.

'I don't think you can be everything to everyone. I've learned that you should do what you're good at really well.'

NIKKI TIBBLES

FLORIST

As the owner of Wild at Heart, Nikki Tibbles is one of London's most sought-after florists, and her vibrant five-storey townhouse in Notting Hill reflects her passion for all things floral. Flowers bloom across furniture, carpets, walls and canvases – this is not a lady who does things by halves.

'I love anything floral, whether it's on a dress or a dressing table,' Nikki explains. 'My style at home is colourful, eclectic and slightly chaotic – although I'm always aiming for organized chaos. I love playing with colour and pattern, on top of pattern, on top of pattern … !'

The interior also combines moody dark backdrops with zingy colour pops, like the sunshine-yellow bookshelves in the otherwise grey kitchen. In the living room, emerald-green rugs are set against dark floral wallpaper and fabrics inspired by Dutch still-life paintings. Collections – of pots, figurines, paintings – appear everywhere, from bedroom walls to hallways, even the bathroom. Pretty floral displays also feature in every room, and Nikki has a vast range of vases, including prized Fulham Pottery by the legendary florist Constance Spry.

When Nikki bought the house in 2000, the interior was anything but stylish. She immediately painted over the apricot walls and made things comfortable, but didn't embark on major renovation works until 13 years later. The basement, which had a separate granny flat, has been transformed into a kitchen with glass doors out to the garden. The ground floor now has a cosy den at one end and a studio at the other,

ABOVE AND OPPOSITE Nikki spotted the 'Dark Floral' wallpaper by Ellie Cashman on Instagram, and had the design printed on velvet for the curtains. The porcelain insect vases are a limited edition by Thomas Eyck. The sofa is by Knoll.

'My style at home is eclectic and slightly chaotic – but I'm always aiming for organized chaos!'

while the whole of the first floor contains a more formal reception room. Bedrooms and bathrooms are tucked away on the floors above. A half-landing has been turned into a reading nook with a plump pink armchair and rainbow-bright rug.

Nikki first tried her hand at floristry in the early 1990s when she offered to do the flowers for a friend's wedding. She was working in advertising at the time and looking for a change in career direction. 'I'm creative, but I can't paint or write,' she explains, 'and I realized that flowers were the perfect medium to express myself.'

Somehow, she also finds time to campaign for her animal welfare charity, the Wild at Heart Foundation. 'We aim to reduce the world's 600 million stray dog population by providing funding and support to rescue projects, organizing neutering programmes

and delivering education initiatives,' Nikki says. 'I'm very proud of the work we have achieved.'

Nikki herself is the owner of five large rescue dogs, which bound around the house. 'My perfect weekend is spent at home surrounded by close friends and family, cooking, eating and then going for a long stroll with my five beautiful dogs,' she says. 'It's bliss!'

ABOVE RIGHT The cool greys of the kitchen units and marble worktop are enlivened by a punchy blind in 'Etamine' by Zimmer + Rohde. The 'Caravaggio' pendant lights are from SCP.

OPPOSITE A 'Cherry' pendant light by Nika Zupanc for Qeeboo and oversized woven wicker vases add a playful touch to the dining room.

THIS PAGE Nikki has vases and pots in every room of the house – even the bathroom, where her collection of mantel vases is displayed by the freestanding tub.

OPPOSITE Even Nikki's bed has a floral theme. 'I wanted the bedrooms to be much calmer, with a plush fabric on the beds,' she says.

CAMILLE WALALA

ARTIST AND DESIGNER

Spending time with Camille Walala in her one-bedroom flat in Haggerston, East London, makes one long to be as brave and uninhibited as she is in her design choices, rejecting 'tasteful' furnishings to harness instead the joyful exuberance of childhood and live more colourfully.

Using colour and pattern as her medium, the London-based French print designer creates a big impact, whether applying her motifs to side plates or to the sides of buildings. Since founding her studio after graduating from the University of Brighton in 2009, her technicolour patterns have adorned everything from shoes and rugs to Easter eggs and school playgrounds.

Camille uses the walls of her rented flat as a test canvas for her designs, which appear everywhere you turn. Fortunately, the landlord gave her carte blanche to decorate it how she pleased – as long as she returns it to its magnolia blandness before she leaves. In another stroke of good fortune, her next-door neighbour was a decorator, who she enlisted to create a whitewashed blank canvas, ready to receive the Camille treatment.

As well as the eye-popping murals applied to every surface, each piece of furniture, textile and decorative accessory has been chosen or customized to play its part in the pattern play. Floors have been covered with geometric rugs, handblock-printed fabric transformed into curtains and a kitchen towel holder repurposed to house stacks of zingy bangles on the dressing table.

ABOVE LEFT AND RIGHT Camille's passion for pattern extends from her personal style to her home; graphic stripes can be seen on everything from miniature pots to rugs, as well as zipping along walls.

OPPOSITE Camille has transformed the uninspiring backdrop of a rental flat in Hackney into a feast for the eyes.

Much of the furniture has been painted in searingly bright primary hues. Flatpack basics and charity-shop finds have been upcycled, with clashing hues that recall the Memphis Group in the 1980s. The patterns of the South African Ndebele people and works by painters such as Auguste Herbin are also recurring influences.

'My mum's house was full of colour and she loved African patterns,' says Camille, who grew up in Provence. 'My father always had Memphis-style pieces in his home. I love their graphic playfulness: it reminds me to have fun with my own work and bring a smile to people's faces.'

Camille has transformed urban landscapes across the world, for clients that range from Nike and Armani to Nintendo and Facebook. She started out closer to home in East London, decorating nightclub interiors, cafés and shopfronts around Shoreditch – and has even created a giant 'bouncy castle' beside Liverpool Street Station to help frenetic city workers alleviate stress.

'I wanted to bring a bit more colour and pattern to the sea of grey in the area,' says Camille of the project, although the statement could equally apply to anything she turns her hand to. The future looks bright for this purveyor of positivity, and somehow it seems unlikely her landlord will be painting the apartment magnolia again when Camille decides it's time to move on.

ABOVE LEFT AND RIGHT Pattern and colour spills forth from inside wardrobes and down to floor cushions and carpets.

OPPOSITE A zingy yellow mural adds pep to the bedroom. The DIY approach and Ikea cabinet and mirror prove that good design can be democratic.

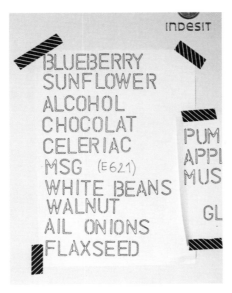

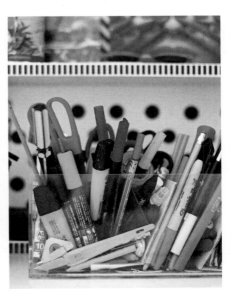

THIS PAGE Every surface – from shelves to floors, even the fridge – has been covered in Camille's punchy patterns. She uses paint, tape, stickers and marker pens to make them, 'just whatever comes to hand'.

OPPOSITE The striking desk has also received the Camille treatment.

REBECCA LOUISE LAW

INSTALLATION ARTIST

Moving to Columbia Road in Shoreditch was something of a Christmas miracle for artist Rebecca Louise Law and her actor husband Andrew in 2007. Having been renting in nearby Bethnal Green, their landlord served notice just a few days before the holidays.

'We managed to find a flat on Columbia Road the next day, but we had to make a decision immediately,' Rebecca recalls. 'It was above a betting shop and stank of cigarettes, but thankfully the smoking ban came into effect soon after.'

Five years later they moved four doors down ('all the neighbours have seen every single thing I own, because we carried it all down the street') to their current home, which has a shopfront at street level that Rebecca uses as a gallery space for her art.

With its longstanding flower market, Columbia Road is a fitting address: Rebecca creates ethereally beautiful installations with flowers that slowly decay and fade over time. She prefers not to label herself as a florist or floral artist, but as an artist who uses flowers as a medium. Her works are designed to last for decades rather than a few days.

'Using the flowers as an art material hasn't been easy,' she says. 'They are ephemeral objects, and people immediately associate flowers with a short lifespan. I have to change that in the viewer's mind when they approach the work, so that the flower isn't necessarily the subject; the experience is the subject.'

Rebecca sews each flower with copper wire to preserve it, ensuring that her installations could – theoretically – exist indefinitely. As the pigment is bleached out, the blooms fade to hues of yellow, orange and cream.

ABOVE LEFT AND RIGHT Surprisingly, the velvet and leather sofa is from a high-street homewares store; a Persian carpet in the living room.

OPPOSITE A ground-floor reception room serves as a gallery space where Rebecca displays examples of her melancholically beautiful work.

'The flower is a form within a massive sculpture, so there isn't really a sadness to it — it's more a celebration of preserving it and keeping it alive.'

Several rooms of the house are decorated with examples of Rebecca's work, which run the gamut from very small to huge installations. In the hallway, for instance, antique vitrines contain a mesmerizing display of flowers and oceanic treasures, each a cabinet of curiosities in miniature.

'I was obsessed with collecting shells as a child – they were my first love,' says Rebecca. 'I see them as flowers of the sea. Most of the shells you'll see in sculptures are ones that I have collected over the years. The really small things – the tiny sculptures and paintings – that's just me needing to just paint or make something. It's good for my soul.'

Her work is well suited to the house, which has retained its original 19th-century layout. The floors are uneven, and the fireplaces (a relatively recent addition) are 'wonky'. The atmosphere is still and timeless.

Rebecca loves the sort of sturdy, dark wood furniture that has fallen out of fashion. 'Some of the furniture is very old and precious, but most is just from charity shops,' she says. 'I managed to get nearly everything else for under £50.'

Although Rebecca is thrifty, there are some indulgent touches, such as a mini-parlour in the roomy bathroom. 'We put these cocktail chairs in here so we can have a chat while one of us is in the bath,' she explains. 'It's our time to unwind and wash away the stresses of the day.'

ABOVE LEFT AND RIGHT A painting by Rebecca hangs above her bed; an antique vitrine contains one of her pieces in the hallway. The colours slowly fade and become sepia-toned.

OPPOSITE Cocktail chairs add a sumptuous touch to the bathroom.

THIS PAGE The kitchen has many original features, lending it a charming, country-cottage look. Rebecca has repurposed the hearth as valuable storage space.

OPPOSITE Rebecca has deliberately kept the courtyard garden largely flower-free, preferring an evergreen sanctuary from her work and the bustle of London life.

SERAFINA SAMA

FASHION DESIGNER

Serafina Sama's Italian heritage is reflected in
her opulent West London home. Among the rich
tapestries, gilded floor lamps and velveteen seating
are fashionable flourishes, including vintage
Louis Vuitton trunks and a carpet by Vivienne
Westwood, emblazoned with magnolia flowers.

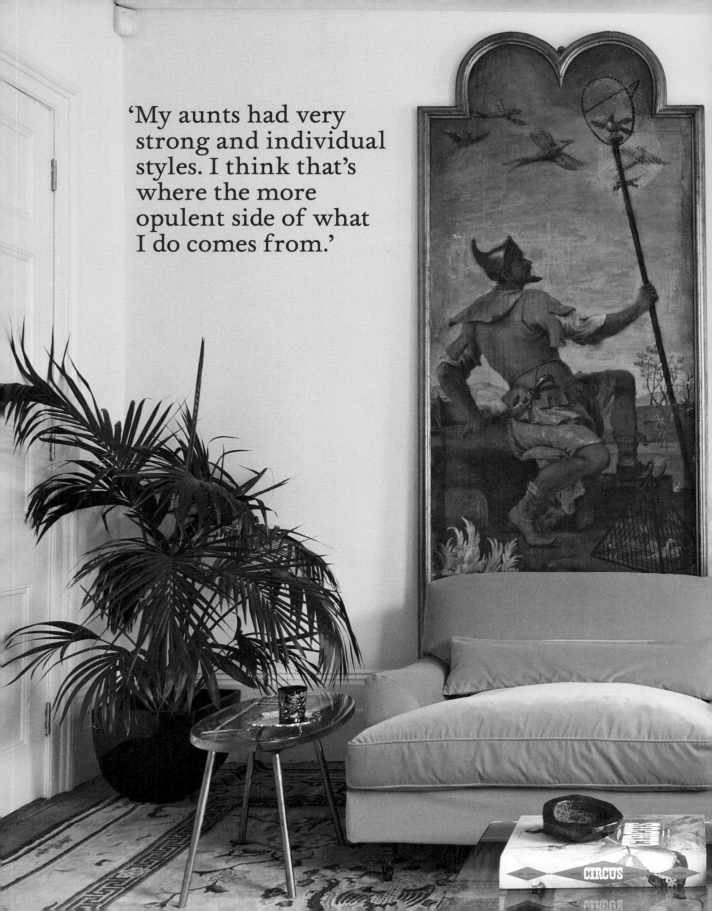

'My aunts had very strong and individual styles. I think that's where the more opulent side of what I do comes from.'

These two loves – Italy and fashion – have also come together in Serafina's fashion label Isa Arfen, which she launched in 2012. 'It's an anagram of my name, but Isa was also my maternal grandmother's name, so it's a little homage to her,' she says. 'I liked the idea of something that sounded like a person's name, but was not mine.'

The aesthetic, too, is very much influenced by women in her family, particularly her two glamorous maternal aunts. Growing up in Ravenna, northeast Italy, Serafina drew 'thousands' of sketches of girls in dresses inspired by her aunts' eccentric style.

'They had very strong and individual styles – one was into vintage and ethnic costumes, colourful pieces and oversized jewelry,' she explains. 'I think that's where the more opulent side of what I do has come from.'

Serafina has applied the same mix-and-match approach to the home she shares with her husband and young son. The master bedroom is awash with statement pieces, with a huge antique French tapestry hanging behind a vintage Italian bed.

Along the hallway, a spare bedroom has been transformed into a glamorous bathroom and dressing area, complete with an Art Deco-style vanity unit, geometric floor tiles and Kentia palms. The freestanding bath sits on a raised platform in the window, adding to the feeling of old-world decadence.

ABOVE LEFT Vintage Louis Vuitton cases and fashion accessories in a corner of the dining room reflect Serafina's sartorial flair.

OPPOSITE Kentia palms and a bold carpet by Vivienne Westwood for the Rug Company give the dining room a botanical spin.

Both bedroom and bathroom would provide a fitting backdrop to one of Serafina's fashion presentations, which eschew a minimalist catwalk in favour of an atmospheric tableau created with set designer Andrea Cellerino.

Serafina moved to London aged 17, to study first architecture and then, after persuading her parents that fashion wasn't too frivolous a discipline, fashion design and marketing at Central St Martins. After graduating, she worked in Paris for two years as a design assistant for Chloé, before moving back to London.

While juggling motherhood and working as a consultant for Acne, Louis Vuitton and Charlotte Olympia, Serafina designed a small collection of easy-to-wear summer dresses that were an instant hit with friends. Demand grew through word of mouth, and Isa Arfen was born.

'I liked the idea of creating a small wardrobe of pieces that were realistic and relatable, that anyone could wear again and again,' Serafina explains. 'I see the pieces on my aunt, who is now in her seventies, and she looks amazing.'

She can also be spotted wearing her own sophisticated separates while hunting for vintage treasures at Portobello Market on Friday mornings. Weekends are spent with family, 'cooking, relaxing, hopefully seeing an exhibition, buying flowers and maybe shopping for antiques'. Serafina may be an Italian eccentric at heart, but London is very much home.

OPPOSITE AND ABOVE RIGHT The capacious bathroom also functions as a dressing area, complete with a glamorous trunk-style vanity unit.

OPPOSITE The master bedroom channels high-octane Italian glamour. An antique tapestry provides a sumptuous backdrop for the teal-velvet upholstered bed.

KEVIN TORRE

FASHION AND INTERIOR DESIGNER

Kevin Torre's home, a tiny studio in a disused school near Paddington Station, proves emphatically that you don't need lots of space, money or even time to create a striking interior. Sometimes imagination and the bravery to bring a bold vision to life are all that's needed.

Like a continually evolving art installation, the ceiling and walls of Kevin's flat are covered with murals that change along with his moods.

'I just need to express myself all the time, so painting on the walls was the quickest way to bring my thoughts to life,' he says. 'Some of them are more deep and dark. I like to cover every part of the room, even the ceiling. To me, a blank space is a missed opportunity to create art or a vignette with beautiful objects.'

As the visual manager of Heal's, one of London's most iconic furniture and design stores, Kevin is adept at quickly conjuring a mood, transforming shop floors and windows with head-turning displays of furniture. But while his work is about creating polished scenes filled with objects that customers want to take home, his own apartment is more edgy and experimental.

'It's a kind of bohemian style with a touch of opulence,' he says of the interior decor. 'I don't like things to be too perfect, too square.'

Kevin's fellow residents in what can best be described as a just-about-official squat are similarly creative (costume designers, architects, dancers), and often come together to cook and eat in the communal kitchens.

'It's an incredibly inspiring building that's full of energy,' Kevin says. 'It was a school in the past, and it's really interesting to walk the hallways and imagine all the things that people learned here.' Of his neighbours, he adds: 'We are like a family.'

ABOVE LEFT Kevin in front of one of the murals he created in his ever-changing studio apartment.

OPPOSITE A striking vignette created by Kevin, who applies the skills honed as a visual merchandiser for fashion and homeware stores to conjure up head-turning drama with humble materials.

'I need to express myself all the time. Painting on the walls was the quickest way to bring my thoughts to life.'

Kevin's love of design and travel was nurtured by his grandfather, who was a chef on the ocean liner *SS France* in the 1960s, and lived between New York and Le Havre, where his grandparents' house was full of photographs and travel mementos.

'The atmosphere in the house was magical,' he remembers. 'My grandparents also had a little house in Cannes, and the light there was wonderful. They both inspired me to really look at the world from a very young age.'

Though his work involves travel and keeping in tune with emerging trends, both of which he loves, Kevin is happiest tucked up in bed picturing all of the things that he could change in his private universe: a new colour for the ceiling, perhaps, or brighter upholstery fabric for the love-seat sofa, his most prized possession.

Sadly, Kevin will soon have to dismantle his living artwork and move to a more conventional shared home, as the school – and its community – is to be bulldozed to make way for scores of 'luxury' apartments that are unaffordable for the young creatives who have made a home there.

Like many, Kevin is moving out to the far reaches of the capital, taking his vitality and energy with him.

ABOVE LEFT The swirling statement headboard provides a strong focal point and gives the bed decorative appeal in this tiny studio apartment.

OPPOSITE Kevin's immaculately curated clothing rails: there was no space for a wardrobe in the room.

SOPHIE ASHBY

INTERIOR DESIGNER

'My parents have moved house an obscene number of times,' says interior designer Sophie Ashby. 'I spent the whole of my childhood viewing houses, and by the time I was 19 we'd lived in 14 different ones. So I was interested in property from a young age.'

MUSEE MATISSE NICE

Having decided early on that she wanted to be an architect or an interior designer, she studied history of art in the UK, followed by a term at Parsons design school in New York. Back in London, she worked for two interior designers, before making the gutsy decision to set up her own practice, aged just 25.

'I thought I'd just try my best to turn over a couple of projects a year,' says Sophie, who started out with her laptop in a coffee shop. 'I just wanted the freedom to be able to develop my own style. By that point I had figured out what I liked.'

Other people also liked her fresh take on interiors, and within three years she had a team of 11 people working on projects – from hotels to new-build lofts and plush private residences – in London and Cape Town, where she lived until the age of 12 (her mother is South African).

Sophie's own home – a one-bedroom flat in Notting Hill that she shares with her boyfriend, fashion designer Charlie Casely-Hayford – is rented, constraining her ability to make permanent changes. Nonetheless, it is a masterclass in how accessorizing can transform a white cube into a home.

Her peripatetic childhood meant that Sophie got 'a lot of experience of rearranging my room to make it comfortable'. Her design formula of earthy, desaturated colours, judiciously placed hits of pattern and 'lots of plants and art' is simple and very effective.

OPPOSITE Sophie collects photographic art as it is relatively affordable, and often uses land- or seascapes in her interior-design schemes to create 'a window into a beautiful world'. The chair is upholstered in a fabric from Pierre Frey.

'For me, the art is what's most important,' says Sophie, who is also a Young Patron of the Royal Academy. 'When I design a room, I start with an artwork and take inspiration from the colours.'

While she usually has generous budgets at her disposal, she acknowledges that buying art can be expensive and daunting. The wall of art above the L-shaped sofa in her own apartment has been put together thriftily – framed posters, prints and pages from secondhand books all make an appearance.

Sophie also enjoys trawling vintage markets and antiques shops, and numerous pre-loved finds are dotted about her home, including a mid-century armchair, reupholstered in a printed Pierre Frey linen that reflects her love of Africa, along with beaded South African bowls and Moroccan Beni Ourain rugs.

'I love the foraging and sourcing element of my work and going to markets,' she explains. 'I don't do interior design in the most commercially minded way. I go to far too many different places per project – for some projects there might be 300 different suppliers. The way that I think about it is that I'm a collector, and I just try to imagine that it's my house.'

Judging by Sophie's own cool, comfortable apartment, she should keep doing what she loves.

ABOVE LEFT AND RIGHT Decorative touches in the kitchen include travel finds such as African sculptures and pots.

OPPOSITE Sophie's home office, complete with a moodboard of family photographs.

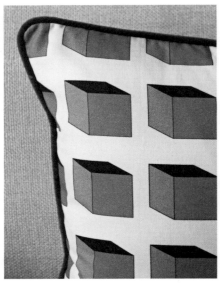

THIS PAGE 'The idea of having my own shop or curated space is probably what I'm aiming for,' says Sophie. 'That's the dream. I love collecting beautiful things.'

OPPOSITE The bedroom has a more traditional feel with a wrought-iron bedstead and shabby-chic furniture. 'The first interior designer I worked for, Victoria Fairfax, did big country homes with really classical interior design,' Sophie explains. 'I got a very good understanding of antiques from her: she had an amazing sense of colour.'

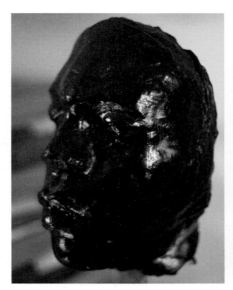

'The art is what's most important. When I design a room, I start with an artwork and take inspiration from the colours.'

DANIELA CECILIO

FASHION TECH ENTREPRENEUR

'Everywhere in London feels so small and the lack of space was suffocating me,' says Brazilian-born Daniela Cecilio, as she walks through the open-plan living area of her capacious apartment. 'In Brazil, even if you're very poor you can still have a decent amount of space to live in.'

Even after making the capital her home for several years, Daniela couldn't shake the feeling of being hemmed-in, particularly as the home she previously shared with her husband Jose Neves, founder of the fashion e-tailer Farfetch.com, was 'lovely but tiny'.

The Victorian property with its stacked, boxy rooms felt too enclosed, and Daniela sought the luxury of space and the ability to spread out. While she was abroad, she came across this loft-style apartment in Islington on busy Upper Street on a 'dodgy-looking property website' and asked Jose to view it.

'He had a look and made an offer on the spot,' Daniela says. 'By the time I came back we were ready to move in. I hadn't seen the place, so I was very nervous.'

After entering the Georgian property via a dramatically dark hallway, the soaring double-height ceiling and huge Palladian windows come as a pleasant surprise. Formerly a ballroom, the space was redeveloped in the mid-2000s and a mezzanine floor added to house two bedrooms, each with their own bathroom. Wrapping around one side of the flat, the elevated area allows the living space to benefit from the building's generous proportions.

ABOVE The kitchen units conceal the staircase up to the mezzanine and a home office area. Much of the crockery was a gift from Daniela's mother-in-law.

OPPOSITE The tabletop, made from a 100-year-old church door, is an eBay find. The mirrorball lights are by Tom Dixon.

'It's a great place for entertaining. When we have parties, the Italian restaurant next door brings all the food up the fire escape.'

The division and concealment of space has been smartly done throughout; you wouldn't realize that the staircase was tucked behind the run of built-in storage in the back of the living area, for example, and there are folding shutters on the mezzanine, which can open up or close off the space.

'Part of the reason we fell in love with the flat is that it has been very thoughtfully renovated, with lots of great details that I would never have thought of adding,' says Daniela. 'If you're upstairs you can't hear what's going on down here once you close the shutters, because they've been soundproofed.'

Furnishing the space presented a challenge. Some of the couple's existing pieces felt too small, and so two key new purchases – an impressive dining table that seats 10 and shelving that also serves as a room divider – were bespoke commissions. The table is topped by an old church door, bought on eBay, and the shelving unit was made in Portugal, where Daniela and Neves have a second home.

The rest of the furniture is a mix of design classics, vintage one-offs and colourful travel finds. As the founder of the fashion app Asap54 – a 'shoppable mix of Instagram and Shamzan' – Daniela is constantly travelling, making time at home all the more valuable.

OPPOSITE Of the reading nook, Daniela says, 'I always wanted this corner to be a place that you could meditate in the morning.'

PREVIOUS PAGES The Vitra armchairs in the living area are a re-edition of a classic 1939 design, while the vintage drinks trolley came from One Columbia Road. The rug was picked up during a trip to Morocco.

HAYLEY NEWSTEAD

FLORIST AND INTERIOR DESIGNER

Hayley Newstead's small-but-perfectly formed flat is located in a converted 1930s building designed by Wallis, Gilbert & Partners – the architectural practice behind many iconic Art Deco buildings in the UK – but was in need of a makeover after unsympathetic renovations in previous decades.

Hayley, founder of bijoux store Absolute Flowers & Home in Little Venice, has made a striking combination of the natural and the manmade her trademark. Her chic clientele includes the fashion house Louis Vuitton and actress-turned-wellbeing guru Gwyneth Paltrow, and she is also on speed dial to add floral flourishes to Madonna's London home and styled the singer's dressing rooms during her last three world tours.

Her design for the interior of cult vegan restaurant Farmacy in West London is elegant and rustic, thanks to a palette of natural materials, soothing colours and a profusion of leafy plants. Vegetation was also used to fashion many of the furnishings, from the high-backed rattan chairs and ornate bamboo screens to the brass-edged tables with intricate seagrass inlay.

Her own flat in Marylebone may not be decorated in 'jungalow' style – there's surprisingly little in the way of houseplants or flowers here – but the skilfully layered rooms demonstrate that Hayley knows how to blend colour and texture with structure.

A plush new bathroom has replaced the avocado suite, the tiny dated kitchen has been upgraded and extended and the pine flooring replaced with oak parquet. She also incorporated plenty of storage, 'stealing' space where she could, and cleverly extended the

ABOVE AND OPPOSITE The colours and materials of the bijoux kitchen echo the living and dining areas, creating a cohesive visual flow throughout the flat. Portraits of Marilyn Monroe add to the overtly feminine mood of the interior.

wall of the bedroom out into the living room to create wardrobe space. 'It's impossible to live in a small space without somewhere to put your stuff, so storage was key,' she says.

Hayley has done a lot more than just adding in her 'stuff'; the interior design is as polished as the floorplan is practical. The apartment is a resolutely feminine space, as two framed photographs of Marilyn Monroe in the living room attest. To stop things looking too sweet, the colour palette of dusty neutrals and blush pinks is offset with black lacquered furniture and exposed concrete pillars.

The furniture is a mix of old (vintage treasures from Parisian flea markets and London antiques shops) and new (inexpensive high-street finds). There are many glamorous French and Italian pieces from the 1960s and '70s, and rich detailing, including brass door handles on the buff kitchen cabinets and stripes of fringing zipping across curtains and lampshades, give simple backdrops a lift.

The snug has been designed as a cosier evening space with black walls, slubby silk curtains and moss-green velvet upholstery. A brass étagère acts a modern-day cabinet of curiosities – one of many curated displays in the apartment. Naturally, there are lots of vases, and blooms come and go with the seasons. Coral peonies are a spring favourite, because 'it's impossible not to be seduced by their beauty' – just like Hayley's glamorously appointed home.

OPPOSITE The snug is a chic evening space. During the day, the TV blends seamlessly with the black walls – a fact that Hayley loves.

THIS PAGE AND OPPOSITE The buff-coloured bedroom is brimming with glamorous details, including a padded velvet headboard, 1970s brass wall art and vintage Italian pendant light.

FYODOR GOLAN

FASHION DESIGNERS

A vase of impossibly beautiful orchids sits on
the dining table of Fyodor Podgorny and Golan
Frydman's Clerkenwell home. On stepping closer,
it becomes apparent that the flowers are fake and
paint-splattered: an acid-bright re-imagining
of the natural order of things.

'We like to combine natural materials with synthetic things,' explains Golan, who, together with life and work partner Fyodor, designs under the moniker Fyodor Golan. 'We explore that tension between what is traditionally perceived as beautiful and the increasing digitalization and plastification of the way we live now.'

The couple's fashion designs are bright and upbeat on the surface, but there is a brooding undercurrent to their work and the themes they explore often relate to the tipping point between childhood and adolescence.

Their home is also filled with flashes of vivid colour and quirky displays, yet when the duo moved into their warehouse apartment seven months previously it was effectively a sleek, bare canvas. The bare bones were in place as the previous occupant was

an architect who had reworked the space and introduced clever storage, interesting surface textures (polished plaster, wood panelling, sliding leather doors) and the odd characterful touch (note the fruit-crate shelving in the kitchen).

It was exactly the sort of calm, sophisticated backdrop that many people would have been happy to live with, gradually introducing decoration over time. Not so this pair, who swiftly stamped their own colourful mark on the place.

OPPOSITE Fluoro 'Louis Ghost' chairs by Philippe Starck for Kartell and an oversized industrial light-fitting in the dining area.

'I'm very impatient and need things to be done this second,' says Fyodor. 'In the space of a few days we knew what we needed to do, what to buy and what to build.'

And so they set about doing it. Fyodor created the giant moodboard that covers the entire length of one wall of the apartment, including the front door, and hung canvases covered in layers of fluoro tape on the walls and mobiles from the ceiling. Golan made the more solid pieces, including the roughly hewn dining table (offset with neon chairs of Fyodor's choosing) and a shelving unit that houses their books and travel finds.

The moodboard reflects this frenetic pace of change and their current inspirations, although many of the elements – those that reflect family and career history – are unchangeable. A faded family snap of Fyodor as a child in Latvia hangs near a

high-gloss photo of a model wearing an Alexander McQueen dress embellished with embroidery designed by Golan during his time working with the legendary designer. Fyodor, meanwhile, has served in the ateliers of Raf Simons in Belgium and Issey Miyake in Japan.

'We did the whole apartment in five days,' says Golan. 'In our work life, we have four months to produce a collection and create an entire universe around it, from finding the inspiration, to sourcing materials and making the clothes. And then it all starts again.'

OPPOSITE Wooden wardrobes, polished plaster ceilings and leather-clad sliding doors make for a simple yet sophisticated bedroom. 'It used to be as colourful as the rest of the flat and gave me nightmares,' says Fyodor. 'Now we sleep peacefully.' The sliding door is also a nifty space-saving solution in the compact bathroom.

DIRECTORY

Sophie Ashby 250
[studio] Grand Union Studios,
332 Ladbroke Grove,
London W10 5AD
instagram.com/studioashby
twitter.com/studioashby
studioashby.com

Basso & Brooke 148
Bruno Basso & Christopher Brooke
instagram.com/bassoandbrooke
twitter.com/bassoandbrooke
bassoandbrooke.com

Lee Broom 108
[shop] 95 Rivington Street,
Shoreditch, London EC2A 3AY
instagram.com/leebroom
twitter.com/leebroom
leebroom.com

Adam Brown 178
[shop] 24 Sackville Street,
Mayfair, London W1S 3DS
instagram.com/orlebarbrown
twitter.com/orlebarbrown
orlebarbrown.com

Daniela Cecilio 260
twitter.com/dandacecilio
asap54fashionconcierge.com

Clements Ribeiro 140
Suzanne Clements & Inacio Ribeiro
[office] Palladium House,
1–4 Argyll Street,
Soho, London W1F 7LD
instagram.com/clementsribeiro
twitter.com/clementsribeiro
clementsribeiro.com

Carina Cooper 158
[agent] David Higham Associates
davidhigham.co.uk

Chris Dyson 24
[office] 74 Commercial Street,
Spitalfields, London E1 6LY
instagram.com/chrisdysonarchitects
twitter.com/chrisdysonarch
chrisdyson.co.uk

Alex Eagle 72
[studio] 6-10 Lexington Street,
Soho, London W1F 0LB
instagram.com/eagletta
twitter.com/eagletta
alexeagle.co.uk

Fyodor Golan 278
Fyodor Podgorny & Golan Frydman
[studio] Somerset House,
West Water Gate,
South Wing, Victoria Embankment,
London WC2R 1LA
instagram.com/fyodorgolan
twitter.com/fyodor_golan
fyodorgolan.co.uk

Matilda Goad 100
instagram.com/matildagoad
matildagoad.com

Alice Gomme 44
facebook.com/alice.gomme.3

Gillian Hyland 168
instagram.com/gillianhyland
twitter.com/gillian_hyland
gillianhyland.com

Rebecca Louise Law 220
[gallery] 100 Columbia Road,
London E2 7QB
instagram.com/rebeccalouiselaw
twitter.com/rebeccallaw
rebeccalouiselaw.com

Caroline Legrand 62
instagram.com/carolinelegranddesign
carolinelegranddesign.com

Nina Litchfield 52
instagram.com/ninalitchfieldstudios
ninalitchfield.com

Jessica McCormack 82
[shop] 7 Carlos Place,
Mayfair, London W1K 3AR
instagram.com/jessicamccormackdiamonds
jessicamccormack.com

Laura Myers 130
[studio] Unit 7/8, 7 Imperial Road,
Fulham, London SW6 2AG
ateaoceanie.com

Hayley Newstead 268
[shop] 12-14 Clifton Road,
Little Venice, London W9 1SS
instagram.com/hayleynewstead
absoluteflowersandhome.com

Owen Pacey 34
[studio] 193–195 City Road,
Shoreditch, London EC1V 1JN
instagram.com/renaissancelondon
twitter.com/londonfireplace
renaissancelondon.com

Serafina Sama 230
[studio] Unit PL22, Pall Mall Deposit,
124–128 Barlby Road,

Ladbroke Grove, London W10 6BL
instagram.com/isa_arfen
twitter.com/isa_arfen
isaarfen.com

Francis Sultana 92
[studio and showroom]
2–4 King Street, St James's,
London SW1Y 6QP
instagram.com/francis_sultana
twitter.com/francissultana
francissultana.com

Nikki Tibbles 198
[shop] 30 Pimlico Road,
Belgravia, London SW1W 8LJ
instagram.com/nikkitibbleswildatheart
twitter.com/wildathearthq
wildatheart.com
wildatheartfoundation.org

Kevin Torre 240
instagram.com/kevintorreldn
kevin-torre.com

Camille Walala 210
instagram.com/camillewalala
twitter.com/camille_walala
camillewalala.com

Matthew Williamson 188
[office] Studio 10–11, 135 Salusbury Road,
Kilburn, London NW6 6RJ
instagram.com/matthewwilliamson
twitter.com/MWWorld
matthewwilliamson.com

Hubert Zandberg 116
[studio] Studio 5.18, Grand Union Studios,
332 Ladbroke Grove, London W10 5AD
instagram.com/hubertzandberginteriors
hzinteriors.com

On the cover: *Front, clockwise from top left* Striking teal-blue walls in Gillian Hyland's Clapton flat; the organized bohemia of Matthew Williamson's bright-pink hallway; *Back, left to right* Carina Cooper's Notting Hill mews home; Alex Eagle's exquisitely curated loft-style apartment in Soho.

First published in the United Kingdom in 2018
by Thames & Hudson Ltd, 181A High Holborn, London WC1V 7QX

The New Creative Home: London Style © 2018 Thames & Hudson Ltd
Text © 2018 Talib Choudhry
Photographs © 2018 Ingrid Rasmussen (ingridrasmussen.com)

Designed by Anna Perotti

British Library Cataloguing-in-Publication Data
A catalogue record for this book is available from the British Library

ISBN 978-0-500-51922-6

Printed and bound in China by Toppan Leefung Printing Limited

To find out about all our publications, please visit
www.thamesandhudson.com. There you can subscribe to our
e-newsletter, browse or download our current catalogue,
and buy any titles that are in print.